Bridge Odds for Practical Players

Backing outsiders has ruined many a punter at the bridge table as well as at the race track. Few players have any idea of how to harness the odds to solve the problems that constantly recur. Which is the best line of play? Is it better to finesse or play for the drop? Will the diamonds break? Can the chances be combined? What are the exact odds?

Here at last is a simple guide to these situations. Keeping theory to a minimum, the authors show by means of many practical examples how to calculate the odds and how to come up with the right answer time after time at the bridge table. Anyone who learns to apply the principles set out in this book need never again be accused of playing against the odds.

The authors could hardly be better qualified for their task. Hugh Kelsey has earned a world-wide reputation for accurate bridge analysis and lucid prose, while Michael Glauert is a keen and proficient tournament player who holds the first Chair of Mathematics at the University of East Anglia. The reader can therefore be assured of practical bridge advice based on sound mathematical principles.

ALSO BY HUGH KELSEY

Bridge Odds
for Practical Players

HUGH KELSEY
and
MICHAEL GLAUERT

LONDON
VICTOR GOLLANCZ LTD
in association with Peter Crawley
1980

ISBN 0 575 02799 1

Filmset by Willmer Brothers,
Birkenhead, Merseyside
Printed in Great Britain by
St Edmundsbury Press Limited,
Haverhill, Suffolk

Contents

Introduction

A haze of confusion surrounds the way in which probabilities apply to the play of the cards, and the player seeking guidance is poorly served by bridge literature. Most manuals on card-play give a table showing the probable division of the opponents' cards and a few example hands, it is true, but this barely touches the fringe of the subject. At the other extreme are the scientific tomes on probability theory, well-nigh incomprehensible to anyone but a mathematical genius, and in any case of little use as practical guides.

This book is an attempt to cultivate the neglected middle ground where most of the real problems lie. It is a book about bridge, not about mathematics. But bridge is a game with a mathematical structure, which we ignore at our peril. Before getting to grips with the practical side we look at some fundamental ideas about probabilities, because a misunderstanding in this area is often at the root of a player's reluctance to put his trust in what he has read.

Once we have gone over the ground and uncovered a number of simple (but in some cases novel) principles, we go on to show how the application of these principles enables a player to calculate the odds and come up with the right decision in a wide variety of situations. The emphasis throughout is on practical examples, worked out in detail, with the aim of encouraging the reader to tackle similar problems for himself when he meets them.

Working on this book has certainly clarified our ideas about bridge probabilities. We hope that reading it will help to clarify yours.

I

Facts and Figures

There are a number of popular misconceptions about the operation of the laws of chance. Some take the "law of averages" to mean that if a tossed coin has come down heads nine times running it is more likely than not to come down tails on the tenth throw. This is clearly nonsense, for each toss of the coin is a separate fifty-fifty chance. Others take a more sophisticated line, arguing that if heads have appeared 60 times in 100 tossings tails are likely to predominate in the next 100 tosses—"luck evening out". More nonsense. The coin has no memory and is unaffected by past performance.

A genuine mathematical statement (proved in standard books on probability theory) is that there is only a 5% chance that the number of heads in 100 tosses will fall outside the range 40–60, and a 5% chance that the heads in 10,000 tosses will fall outside the range 4,900–5,100 (i.e. 49%–51%). Although the percentage range has dropped, the difference between the number of heads and tails has a continually increasing range. In fact the range increases like the square root of the number of tosses.

The above statement is concerned with *probability*. We cannot say definitely that all 100 tosses will not give heads. Indeed, how could we? The laws of physics certainly don't prevent such an outcome. It is just very unlikely. The odds are in fact 1 in 2^{100}, or about 1 in 10^{30}. This is far too small a chance to be comprehended. It is over a million times more likely that two people, each selecting a grain of sand at random from the Sahara desert, should chance to pick on the same one.

More realistically, the odds of the heads in 100 tossings falling outside the range 30–70 are about 1 in 15,000. This gives a fair indication of what the true "law of averages" says. Although 1 in 15,000 sounds pretty negligible, it cannot be ignored entirely. It is about the same odds that in the next hand you deal someone will receive a ten-card suit.

Which of these sequences of ten tossings, HHHHHHHHHH or HTTHTHHHTH, do you think you would be more likely to achieve if you carried out the experiment now? In fact they have exactly the same probability, 1 in 2^{10} or 1 in 1024, since each time you toss there is a 50% chance that you will match the given sequence.

With coins, dice or roulette wheels, each trial is unaffected by the previous one. But in dealing out playing cards the situation is different. Once the ace of spades has been dealt to a player, it cannot be distributed again in that deal. This new feature causes certain complications, but it also simplifies matters in some ways.

HOW MANY BRIDGE HANDS?

In bridge we are concerned basically with the ways in which a pack of fifty-two cards may be distributed between four players. Let us start from first principles and work out the number of different hands you may hold. Suppose you deal yourself thirteen cards at random from a well-shuffled pack. There are fifty-two possibilities for your first card. Whatever this is, there are then fifty-one possibilities for the second card, and so on down to forty possibilities for your thirteenth and last card.

The number of ways in which you can receive thirteen cards is therefore given by the product of all the numbers from fifty-two down to forty. This does not represent the number of different hands you can hold, however, because the order in which you receive your thirteen cards is irrelevant. A bridge hand is the same no matter how the cards are arranged. You may receive the ace of spades first and the seven of diamonds second, or vice-versa, but if you end up with the same thirteen cards you will still have the same hand. It is not arrangements (permutations) that we are concerned with but blends (combinations). To arrive at the true figure for the number of different hands you can hold, you need to divide by the number of possible permutations of your thirteen cards. (Incidentally, football pool addicts should note that their "permutations" are, confusingly, what the rest of us call combinations).

Clearly, in arranging your hand, you can place any one of thirteen cards on the left, any one of twelve cards next to it, and so on. The number of different arrangements is given by the product of all the numbers from thirteen down to one, and each of these arrangements is included separately in our previous calculation. The number of different hands of thirteen cards that you may hold is therefore:

$$\frac{52 \times 51 \times 50 \times 49 \times 48 \times 47 \times 46 \times 45 \times 44 \times 43 \times 42 \times 41 \times 40}{13 \times 12 \times 11 \times 10 \times 9 \times 8 \times 7 \times 6 \times 5 \times 4 \times 3 \times 2 \times 1}$$

If you care to cancel out the figures in the divisor and multiply out, you will find that the answer is 635,013,559,600.

It is important to appreciate that none of these 635,013,559,600 hands is more probable than any other. You have an equal chance of receiving either:

♠ A K Q J 10 9 8 7 6 5 4 3 2   ♠ Q 6 3 2
♡ —   ♡ A 6
♢ —   or   ♢ K Q 8 5
♣ —   ♣ 10 9 5

This may come as a surprise to some players. Why, they may ask, have I never held thirteen spades since I have often held the second hand? The answer is that they have almost certainly *not* held the second hand, correct to the last spot-card, although they will have held many similar hands. The shape is familiar, for a 4–4–3–2 pattern is much more common than 13–0–0–0. But any hand of thirteen specified cards is just as unlikely as any other.

Let us have another look at the formidable calculation from the previous page.

$$\frac{52 \times 51 \times 50 \times 49 \times 48 \times 47 \times 46 \times 45 \times 44 \times 43 \times 42 \times 41 \times 40}{13 \times 12 \times 11 \times 10 \times 9 \times 8 \times 7 \times 6 \times 5 \times 4 \times 3 \times 2 \times 1}$$

When writing about combinations it is inconvenient to deal in clumsy expressions containing so many digits. It is customary instead to use a sort of mathematical shorthand involving "factorials". The factorial of a number is the product of every whole number from one up to and including that number. Factorial 5 (usually written as 5!), for example, is $1 \times 2 \times 3 \times 4 \times 5$, or 120.

Using this notation we can reduce the lengthy expression above to $\dfrac{52!}{39! \times 13!}$. Factorial 52 represents the product of all the whole numbers from 1 to 52; factorial 39 is the product of all the numbers from 1 to 39. Cancelling out leaves us with the product of all the numbers from 40 to 52 divided by the product of all the numbers from 1 to 13. The answer, 635,013,559,600, represents the number of possible combinations of 52 things (it doesn't have to be cards) taken 13 at a time. This is often written as $_{52}C_{13}$, giving us the equation:

$$_{52}C_{13} = \frac{52!}{39! \times 13!}$$

From this point it is but a short step to deduce the general formula for finding the number of combinations of "n" things taken "r" at a time. This is:

$$_nC_r = \frac{n!}{(n-r)! \times r!}$$

For practice try six things taken two at a time. When you substitute 6 for n and 2 for r, the formula tells you that:

$$_6C_2 = \frac{6!}{(6-2)! \times 2!} = \frac{6!}{4! \times 2!} = \frac{6 \times 5 \times 4 \times 3 \times 2 \times 1}{4 \times 3 \times 2 \times 1 \times 2 \times 1} = \frac{6 \times 5}{2 \times 1} = 15.$$

In other words you can form fifteen different combinations by taking six things two at a time. This sort of calculation is simple enough to be done mentally, and we shall see later its practical importance for bridge players.

HOW MANY DEALS?

We have calculated the number of possible hands that you can hold, but what about the other three players? Well, thirty-nine cards are still available for the second player, and the number of hands that he may be dealt is $_{39}C_{13} = \dfrac{39!}{26! \times 13!} = 8,122,425,444.$

The number of ways in which the third player may then receive thirteen of the remaining twenty-six cards is $_{26}C_{13} = \dfrac{26!}{13! \times 13!} = 10,400,600.$ Finally, the fourth player has no choice but to pick up the thirteen cards that are left.

Since each of the $_{52}C_{13}$ hands for the first player can be combined with any one of the $_{39}C_{13}$ possibilities for the second player, and so on, we arrive at the total number of possible bridge deals by multiplying all our numbers together as follows:

$$\frac{52!}{39! \times 13!} \times \frac{39!}{26! \times 13!} \times \frac{26!}{13! \times 13!} \times 1 = \frac{52!}{(13!)4}$$

This gives a figure that is likely to cause the brightest of minds to boggle—53,644,737,765,488,792,839,237,440,000.

FOUR COMPLETE SUITS

The question that naturally springs to mind at this stage is, what are the chances of all four players being dealt a complete suit? Well, there are 4! or 24 ways in which each player can receive a complete suit, and division by 24 leaves us with odds of 2,235,197,406,895,366,368,301,559,999 to 1 against. If the entire adult population of the world were to play bridge in every waking moment for ten million years, it would still be ten million to one against one of these perfect deals turning up.

So how can we account for all the newspaper reports of four players in a bridge game each receiving a complete suit? The answer is invariably a joker, not in the pack but amongst the players or, more probably, in the ranks of the kibitzers. It is not too hard to switch a pack without being spotted.

ODDS AGAINST A YARBOROUGH

The use of the $_nC_r$ formula makes it a simple matter to work out the probability of holding a hand of any particular type. All we need do is compare the number of possible hands of this type with the total number of hands we can hold. Suppose we wish to ascertain the odds against holding a Yarborough (a hand containing no card higher than a nine), for instance. There are thirty-two cards below the ten in rank, and we can calculate:

$$_{32}C_{13} = \frac{32!}{19! \times 13!} = 347,373,600$$

Dividing this number into the total number of possible hands (635,013,559,600) gives us 1828. The odds against being dealt a Yarborough are therefore 1827 to 1. It seems that the wily Earl of Yarborough knew what he was doing when he wagered £1000 to £1 against the event.

ALL FOUR ACES

In a similar way we can calculate the chances of receiving a hand with any specified feature, such as all four aces. There is only one way in which a player can hold all four aces, but he must also hold nine of the forty-eight non-aces, and the formula gives us:

$$1 \times {}_{48}C_9 = \frac{48!}{39! \times 9!} = 1,677,106,640$$

When we divide this into 635,013,559,600 we find that the odds against holding all four aces are about 378 to 1.

LUCKY OR UNLUCKY

Many players are convinced that they habitually hold less than their fair share of high cards. You probably know someone afflicted with this malady. For such players the game is a long, uphill battle against their cards as well as against their opponents. But if they would take the trouble to keep accurate records for 10,000 hands (a number an active player will clock up in a couple of years) they might be surprised.

Analysis shows, in much the same way for cards as for coins, that there is only a 5% chance that in the 10,000 hands the number of aces held will fall outside the range 9,830–10,170. More dramatically, there is only one chance in 500 million that the count of aces will fall outside the range 9,500–10,500. If your records over 10,000 hands show a total outside this range, you are fully entitled to consider yourself the unluckiest (or the luckiest) bridge player of all time.

HAND PATTERNS

By applying the $_nC_r$ formula to suit-lengths rather than to special features, it is possible to work out the probability of any particular hand pattern. Suppose, for a start, that you wish to know your chance of being dealt a hand containing precisely five spades. As well as five of the thirteen spades you must hold eight of the thirty-nine non-spades. Since each of the $_{13}C_5$ spade choices may be combined with any one of the $_{39}C_8$ non-spade selections, the total number of hands is:

$$_{13}C_5 \times _{39}C_8 = 79,181,063,676$$

This is 12.31% of the total number of hands that you may hold, so the odds against your receiving exactly five spades are roughly 7 to 1.

It is simple enough to extend the process to all four suits. The total number of hands made up of five spades, three hearts, three diamonds and two clubs, for instance, is:

$$_{13}C_5 \times _{13}C_3 \times _{13}C_3 \times _{13}C_2 = 8,211,173,256$$

This represents a frequency of 1.293%. Of course, that is just one particular 5–3–3–2 pattern with the five cards in spades and the doubleton in clubs. There are twelve possible permutations if we permit the length and the shortage to be in any of the four suits, so the general frequency of the 5–3–3–2 hand pattern is 12 × 1.293% or 15.52%.

Here is a table of the more common hand patterns, arranged in order of frequency.

Pattern	Percentage	Pattern	Percentage
4–4–3–2	21.55	7–3–2–1	1.88
5–3–3–2	15.52	6–4–3–0	1.33
5–4–3–1	12.93	5–4–4–0	1.24
5–4–2–2	10.58	5–5–3–0	.90
4–3–3–3	10.54	6–5–1–1	.71
6–3–2–2	5.64	6–5–2–0	.65
6–4–2–1	4.70	7–2–2–2	.51
6–3–3–1	3.45	7–4–1–1	.39
5–5–2–1	3.17	7–4–2–0	.36
4–4–4–1	2.99	7–3–3–0	.27
		all others	.69

Players unfamiliar with this table may be surprised by one or two of its features. It is worth noting that the most balanced hand pattern, 4–3–3–3, is no higher than fifth in the frequency chart.

SUIT-SUPPORT EXPECTANCY

Suppose you have a five-card spade suit. What are the chances that partner will have three-card support?

Partner can hold three of the eight outstanding spades in $_8C_3$ ways. He can hold ten of the thirty-one outstanding non-spades in $_{31}C_{10}$ ways. The number of hands containing three spades that he can hold is therefore:

$$_8C_3 \times _{31}C_{10} = 2,483,719,240$$

The total number of hands that partner can hold is known to be 8,122,425,444, so the probability of his holding precisely three spades is 30.58%.

The calculation of hand-pattern and suit-support expectancy can be of great interest to system-makers, but it is of little practical value at the bridge table. It is in the next section, where we consider the distribution of the opponents' holdings, that the card player can reap rich rewards.

2

Distribution of Opponents' Cards

It is most important for a bridge player to know how his suits are likely to break, for this is the key to correct play in many situations. The probable division of the enemy cards is again something that can be worked out from the first principles with the help of the $_nC_r$ formula. In these situations you already know the twenty-six cards that have been dealt to your side, and the calculations are easier. Suppose that you and dummy have a total of seven spades in your combined hands. What are the chances that the suit will be divided 3–3 between the opponents?

Well, there are $_6C_3$ ways in which an opponent can hold three spades, and $_{20}C_{10}$ ways in which the rest of his hand can be made up. The number of hands containing three spades that he can hold is therefore $_6C_3 \times _{20}C_{10} = 3,695,120$. Expressing this as a percentage of 10,400,600—the total number of hands the opponent can hold—we see that the probability is 35.53%.

This sort of calculation, while far from difficult, is still too laborious to make at the bridge table, so you will find it helpful to familiarise yourself with the main features of the table that follows.

Probable Division of Opponents' Cards

Cards Outstanding	Division	Probability %	Number of Combinations	Probability of Each Combination %
2	1–1	52.00	2	26.00
	2–0 & 0–2	48.00	2 (1+1)	24.00
3	2–1 & 1–2	78.00	6 (3+3)	13.00
	3–0 & 0–3	22.00	2 (1+1)	11.00
4	2–2	40.70	6	6.78
	3–1 & 1–3	49.74	8 (4+4)	6.22
	4–0 & 0–4	9.56	2 (1+1)	4.78
5	3–2 & 2–3	67.83	20 (10+10)	3.39
	4–1 & 1–4	28.26	10 (5+5)	2.83
	5–0 & 0–5	3.91	2 (1+1)	1.96
6	3–3	35.53	20	1.78
	4–2 & 2–4	48.45	30 (15+15)	1.61
	5–1 & 1–5	14.53	12 (6+6)	1.21
	6–0 & 0–6	1.49	2 (1+1)	.75
7	4–3 & 3–4	62.18	70 (35+35)	.89
	5–2 & 2–5	30.52	42 (21+21)	.73
	6–1 & 1–6	6.78	14 (7+7)	.48
	7–0 & 0–7	.52	2 (1+1)	.26
8	4–4	32.72	70	.47
	5–3 & 3–5	47.12	112 (56+56)	.42
	6–2 & 2–6	17.14	56 (28+28)	.31
	7–1 & 1–7	2.86	16 (8+8)	.18
	8–0 & 0–8	.16	2 (1+1)	.08

This table provides a solid foundation for the study of all problems of probability in the play of the cards.

Figures have a fascination of their own, and before anyone falls completely under the spell of the table of probabilities we had better sound a warning note. These are what are called the "*a priori*" probabilities. They are calculated before the deal, and they are valid only in the absence of information from other sources. On many hands there will be indications from the opponents' bidding, from the opening lead or from the early play, and these may cause the odds to shift dramatically. For the present we shall assume that there are no such indications and go on to examine the figures in more detail.

Naturally it is too much to expect anyone to memorize the complete table, but we do suggest that you make yourself familiar with the highlights. The common and important cases are those where the opponents hold four, five or six cards in your suit, and the probable divisions are summarized below.

When opponents hold four cards, they will be divided 2–2 about 40% of the time, 3–1 (or 1–3) about 50% of the time, 4–0 (or 0–4) about 10% of the time.

When opponents hold five cards, they will be divided 3–2 (or 2–3) about 68% of the time, 4–1 (or 1–4) about 28% of the time, 5–0 (or 0–5) about 4% of the time.

When opponents hold six cards, they will be divided 3–3 about 36% of the time, 4–2 (or 2–4) about 48% of the time, 5–1 (or 1–5) about 15% of the time.

If you glance down the "probability" column in the table, you will notice that when the opponents have an odd number of cards, 3, 5, or 7, the most even possible division has in each case a probability well in excess of 50%. In other words, the suit is likely to break kindly for you.

When the opponents have an even number of cards, 4, 6, or 8, however, the probability of an even division is in each case well below 50%. So try to avoid banking on even breaks in such suits.

An exception arises when the opponents have two cards. Now the even (1–1) break is slightly more probable than 2–0 or 0–2.

It can be useful to know the number of possible combinations

[21]

within each particular division of the enemy cards. This information is therefore given in the table, although by now you are quite capable of working it out for yourself. The numbers in brackets simply indicate that the total number of combinations is the sum of two equivalent sets of combinations that arise when one opponent has length and the other shortage. For example, $(4+4)$ means that there are four ways in which West can have three cards and East a singleton, and four ways in which East can have three cards and West a singleton, giving eight combinations in all.

The probability of each combination is given in order to facilitate the working out of practical problems. If the opponents have five cards including the king, for instance, and you wish to determine the chance of East having the king singleton (one of the ten 4–1 and 1–4 combinations), you can just look along the line and read off the figure—2.83%.

Again, if the opponents have five cards including the queen, you may wish to work out the chance of either opponent having queen doubleton. There are twenty possible 3–2 and 2–3 combinations, and if you care to set them all out you will see that the queen is doubleton in eight of these combinations. (A short cut is to reflect that the chance of an opponent holding a specific card is directly proportionate to the number of cards he holds in the suit. The queen will therefore be doubleton in two-fifths of the 3–2 and 2–3 breaks, i.e. in eight of the twenty combinations.) The probability of finding a doubleton queen is therefore eight times the probability of each combination, $8 \times 3.39 = 27.12\%$. In the rest of the 3–2 and 2–3 breaks, 40.71% of the time, the queen will be accompanied by two other cards.

FINESSE OR DROP

Extracting information from the probability table in this manner, we can set out in tabular form the probability of dropping an enemy honour card.

Distribution of Opponents' Cards

When Opponents Have	Probability of an Honour Card Being		
	Singleton %	Doubleton %	Trebleton %
2 cards	52.00	48.00	—
3 cards	26.00	52.00	22.00
4 cards	12.44	40.70	37.30
5 cards	5.66	27.12	40.71
6 cards	2.42	16.15	35.53
7 cards	.96	8.76	26.90
8 cards	.36	4.28	17.67

This in turn enables us to formulate a general rule for those situations where you have to choose between taking a first-round finesse and playing for the drop. Since a simple finesse is a straight 50% shot, equally likely to succeed or to fail, you should finesse whenever the chance of dropping the honour card is less than 50%. We still assume that there are no indications from the bidding or the play.

When Opponents Have

2 cards — Play for the drop, since there is a 52% chance that the king will fall.

3 or 4 cards — Finesse against the king, but not against the queen or jack. The chance of dropping a bare king is well below 50% in both cases, whereas the chance of dropping a singleton or doubleton queen is 78% when three cards are out and 53% when four cards are out.

5 or 6 cards — Finesse against the king or queen but not against the jack. The chance of dropping a singleton or doubleton queen has fallen below 50%

[23]

7 or 8 cards —Finesse against the king, queen or jack. The chance of bringing down the jack in three rounds has fallen well below 50% in both cases.

Many situations at the bridge table are hedged around with slogans designed to guide players who are unable to think for themselves. Naturally the slogan-merchants could not be expected to leave probabilities alone. The popular jingle, "eight ever, nine never," is intended to mean that with eight cards in a suit you should always finesse for a missing queen, with nine cards you should never finesse. But there are no "evers" or "nevers" in bridge. When you have nine cards, the position is so close that the gleam in an opponent's eye may be enough to decide you in favour of a finesse. When you have eight cards it will generally be right to finesse, although at times the context may be such that you should play for the drop.

SPECIFIC CARDS

The probability table is used mainly for determining the likely division of the cards held by the opponents in a particular suit, but it applies with equal force to the division of any specific cards in the enemy hands. If the opponents hold three aces, for example, in the absence of any bidding inference there is a 78% chance that they will be divided 2–1, a 22% chance that one opponent will have all three.

If two honour cards in a suit are missing, there is a 52% chance that they will be split between the opponents, a 48% chance that the same opponent will have them both. This explains why there is a good chance of making two tricks with the following holding.

4 3 2

A J 10

When you lead twice from dummy and finesse, you will fail to make two tricks only when West has both the king and the queen—24% of the time. You will succeed when the honours are divided (52%) and also when East has them both (24%), giving you an overall chance of 76%.

Similar but not identical chances are available in another common double-finesse position.

4 3 2

A Q 10

If you start with a finesse of the ten, you will fail to make two tricks only when West has both missing honours, 24% of the time. You will make two tricks 52% of the time, when the king and the jack are divided between East and West, and you will make all three tricks in the 24% zone where East has both honours.

4 3 2

A K 10

In this position there is no danger of failing to make two tricks, and again you have a 24% chance of making three tricks by taking the deep finesse against East.

4 3 2

Q J 5

This time the best you can hope for is one trick. There is a 76% chance of success if you lead twice from dummy, since you will fail only when West has both the ace and the king.

CHOOSING A LINE OF PLAY

Let us now consider how a knowledge of basic probabilities can help to determine the best line of play at the bridge table.

[25]

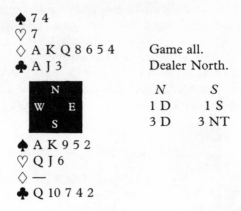

♠ 7 4
♡ 7
◇ A K Q 8 6 5 4   Game all.
♣ A J 3   Dealer North.

N	S
1 D	1 S
3 D	3 NT

♠ A K 9 5 2
♡ Q J 6
◇ —
♣ Q 10 7 4 2

West leads the five of hearts to his partner's ace. East returns the two of hearts to the queen and king. You discard a spade from dummy, and then a diamond as West continues with the three of hearts to the nine and jack. How do you plan the play?

The hearts appear to be divided 5–4, so if the defenders regain the lead they will be able to cash two more heart tricks to defeat the contract. With seven top tricks, you need to develop two more in one of the minor suits without losing the lead. You could try an immediate club finesse, playing the queen and running it if West plays low, or you could go up with the ace of clubs and rely on the diamonds for your extra tricks.

As you know from the probability table, the chance of a 3–3 diamond split is nearly 36%. To that you can add something for the chance of dropping a singleton king of clubs, bringing the chance of success for this line of play up to about 39%. But the club finesse offers a 50% chance and that is the superior play.

Actually, as we shall see when we re-examine the hand in a later chapter, the above analysis is an over-simplification. The true difference between the two lines of play is considerably less than 11%. Nevertheless, when the table of probabilities indicates a wide gap between the chances of two lines of play it is safe to assume that one line is better than the other.

♠ 6 5
♡ A K 8 7 6 2   Love all.
◇ 9 6 4   Dealer South.
♣ 8 2

	S	*N*
	2 C	2 H
N	2 S	3 H
W E	4 C	4 H
S	4 NT	5 D
	6 NT	—

♠ K Q J 10
♡ 4
◇ A K Q J
♣ A K Q 10

West leads the jack of hearts to dummy's ace, East following with the three. How do you try for twelve tricks?

That heart lead was far from friendly. On any other lead you could have knocked out the spade ace and claimed your slam. Now, since you have to go out to the ace of spades, you cannot afford to take a discard on the king of hearts. You have to abandon the heart king on the table and hope to make four club tricks.

The choice lies between two lines of play. You can either lead a club at trick two for an immediate finesse of the ten, or you can leave the clubs alone and play on spades. In the latter case it is too much to expect that a defender will be helpful enough to return a second heart, and in the end you will be reduced to hoping for the jack of clubs to fall under your top honours.

Well, our general finessing rule tells you that when the opponents have seven cards you should finesse against the jack, and a glance at the table on page 23 confirms this. The jack will drop singleton, doubleton or trebleton just under 37% of the time. Clearly the 50% finesse is the better chance.

[27]

Now try your hand at a grand slam.

♠ K 10 8
♡ A 7 6 3
◇ 8 7 4
♣ K 5 4

♠ A Q J 9 3
♡ 5
◇ A K J
♣ A Q J 7

You arrive in a contract of seven spades and West leads the queen of hearts to dummy's ace, East playing the eight. How do you plan the play?

Twelve top tricks are on view, and the straightforward method of play is to rely on the diamond finesse for the thirteenth trick. Draw trumps, cash the ace of diamonds, cross to the king of clubs, and lead a diamond for a finesse of the jack. This line of play has a probability of success of 50.48%, the extra .48% coming from the chance of felling a singleton queen of diamonds in the West hand.

You can do better than that, however, by playing to score a sixth trump trick. Ruff a heart with the jack of spades at trick two, play a club to dummy's king, ruff a heart with the queen of spades, and return the three of spades to dummy's eight. Ruff the fourth heart with the ace of spades, lead the nine of spades to dummy's ten and cash the spade king. You discard the jack of diamonds on this trick and, if all has gone well, the rest of your hand is high.

The dummy reversal succeeds when the trumps are divided 3–2, and the probability table indicates that this will happen 67.83% of the time. The possibility of a first-round club ruff reduces the overall chance of success to 66.82%, but that is still a big improvement on the diamond finesse.

It is worth noting that the initial lead of a trump, the traditional lead against a grand slam, would have left you short of an entry for the dummy reversal, forcing you to fall back upon the diamond finesse.

3

Percentage Play

The knowledge of how the residue of a suit is likely to be divided between the opponents' hands enables us to work out the best way of handling any particular combination of cards in a single suit. There are literally hundreds of common card combinations (the *Official Encyclopaedia of Bridge* lists 656) and it is clearly impossible for us to deal with them all here. And yet, familiarity with these positions is essential. No one can expect to cope successfully with a problem in card combinations unless he has previously met and studied something similar, either at the bridge table or on paper.

What we propose to do in this chapter is to show, through a small but representative number of examples, how the probabilities are calculated in such situations. The reader who understands *why* one line of play is superior to another will be well equipped to tackle similar problems on his own.

The correct way of handling a suit often depends on the number of tricks you need from it. For example:

A K Q 6 5

4 2

That's a useful-looking suit, but suppose that dummy has no outside entry. If you need five tricks from the suit you have no option but to play out the ace, king and queen, hoping for a 3–3 division of the enemy cards. As you know, the 3–3 break has a probability of only 36%, so your prospects are not very bright.

Now suppose that you need only four tricks in the suit and that you can afford to lose a trick to the opponents. The way to maximize your chance of success is to play a low card from dummy on the first round. You will then make four tricks not only when the suit breaks 3–3 but also when it breaks 4–2, giving you a total chance of 84% (36% + 48%).

THE SAFETY PRINCIPLE

This type of play in which a trick is conceded, perhaps unnecessarily, in order to increase the chance of making the number of tricks that you need, is called a "safety play". In effect, you take out insurance against a bad break, the trick given up representing the premium payable on your policy.

To see how rewarding safety play can be, let us put our suit into a complete hand and examine the arithmetic.

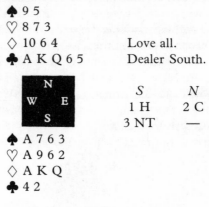

♠ 9 5
♡ 8 7 3
◇ 10 6 4   Love all.
♣ A K Q 6 5   Dealer South.

	S	N
	1 H	2 C
	3 NT	—

♠ A 7 6 3
♡ A 9 6 2
◇ A K Q
♣ 4 2

West leads the two of spades to the king and ace. Now if you play the clubs from the top you will make ten tricks for a score of 430 in thirty-six out of a hundred such deals. In the remaining sixty-four deals you will go one down for a loss of 50, so from your 15,480 points we have to deduct 3,200, leaving you with a profit of 12,280.

However, the opening lead indicates that the spades are 4–3, in which case you can afford to concede a club trick. If you duck a club at trick two, you will make nine tricks for a score of 400 on eighty-four out of a hundred such deals. From your total of 33,600 points we have to deduct 800 for the sixteen times you go one down, leaving a profit of 32,800. Over a hundred deals, therefore, you gain more than 20,000 extra points by employing the safety play.

Sometimes it is possible to achieve absolute security.

A K Q J 4 3

7 2

Again there is no outside entry in dummy, and again if you need all the tricks you have to play out the suit from the top. This time your prospects are much brighter, for there is a 96% chance that the suit will break 3–2 or 4–1.

If you need only five tricks, however, and if you can afford the premium, you can insure against a 5–0 break by ducking on the first round. This gives you a gilt-edged guarantee of five tricks in the suit.

The question is sometimes asked: "Are safety plays that protect against such improbable divisions worth while?" Let us again place the suit in the context of a complete hand.

♠ 7 5 4
♡ 6
◇ A K Q J 4 3   Game all.
♣ 8 6 3   Dealer South.

	N	
W		E
	S	

S	N
1 C	1 D
1 S	3 D
3 NT	—

♠ A 9 8 2
♡ A K 4
◇ 7 2
♣ A 10 7 4

West leads the jack of hearts, East follows with the eight and you win with the king. When you lead the two of diamonds West plays the five.

You have reached the moment of decision. The only thing that can endanger your contract is a diamond void in the East hand, and you can protect yourself completely against this 2% chance by playing a low diamond from dummy. You will then score two hearts, five diamonds, and the black aces for game. Of course, you are giving up all chance of an overtrick, and in a pairs game, where overtricks are vital, you would not dream of making such a safety play.

At rubber bridge or in a team game overtricks are relatively unimportant, but let's check the arithmetic.

If you make the safety play of ducking the first diamond, you will score a vulnerable game instead of going one down two times out of a hundred. This represents two swings of 700 points, a total gain of 1400 over a hundred such deals. However, if you ignore the safety play and cash the top diamonds you will make an overtrick (worth 30 points) on the ninety-six occasions when the suit breaks 3–2 or 4–1, giving a total gain of 2880. The mathematical expectancy over a hundred similar deals, therefore, is that you will be 1480 points to the good if you ignore the safety play.

Figures such as these build up a strong case against marginal safety plays in the eyes of those who confuse arithmetic with bridge. The argument, although mathematically sound, is psychologically naive. It would be valid enough if the game were a contest between computers, influenced solely by mathematical considerations. But bridge is played by creatures of flesh and blood, subject to moods of elation and despair, prone to a loss of morale after a bad result, and this is where the chain of reasoning breaks down.

If you ignore the safety play and fail to make your contract, partner will not be interested in hearing about the overtrick you expect to make on ninety-six similar hands. All he will see is that you have put a cold game on the floor. If not actively disgruntled he will certainly be far from gruntled, and it is long odds that his peevish play and lack of concentration on the next few hands will cost you more than you can ever hope to recoup in overtricks.

Our advice is to forget about overtricks (except at match-point pairs) and concentrate on making your contract as safely as possible. Do not listen to the siren-song of those who decry safety plays. At rubber bridge, fortunately, you can expect to play against the overtrick-fanciers twice as often as you play with them. But keep these match-losers out of your teams at all costs.

Here is another situation where you can cater for a void in either hand.

A K 9 4 3

Q 8 2

To make sure of four tricks, lead low from either hand for a finesse of the eight or nine. If dummy has an outside entry, leading low towards the nine has an edge. Then you will make all five tricks when West has J 10, J 10 x or J 10 x x.

In the next example the lead is with South. There are several outside entries in dummy but none in hand.

10 5 4

A K Q 7 2

The only way to make sure of four tricks is to start by leading the two from hand. If East is void, dummy's ten will be worth a trick. If West is void, the ten will force out the jack and four tricks will be made by finessing twice aginst the eight and nine.

The next combination is often misplayed.

A Q 7 3

8 6 5 4 2

If you need five tricks, of course, you must take a first-round finesse and hope for the best. You will succeed 20% of the time, when the suit breaks 2–2 and the king is with West. The chance of making at least four tricks by this method is 65%, since you will succeed whenever the suit breaks 2–2 and also in half of the 3–1 breaks (when West has the singleton king and when East has a lower singleton).

If the target is four tricks and entries are no problem, however, you can do better by abandoning the attempt to make five tricks. Play the ace on the first round and, if the king does not drop, return to hand in another suit and lead towards the queen. This caters for the possibility of a singleton king in the East hand, increasing your chance of four tricks to 71%.

Guarding against the possibility of a singleton honour can augment your chances in many situations.

A Q 7 6 5 4

J 3

With this combination there is no way of making all six tricks, and the best shot for five tricks is to start with the ace. You will succeed when the suit breaks 3–2 and also when the king is singleton in either hand, giving you about $73\frac{1}{2}\%$. The alternative plays of leading the three for a finesse of the queen and leading low from dummy towards the jack are both about 3% worse.

We saw in the last chapter that when the opponents have five cards including the queen the best chance of avoiding a loser is to finesse against the queen.

6 4 3

A K J 10 9

With the above holding, for instance, you could take a first-round finesse of the nine and, entries permitting, repeat the finesse two more times if necessary. However, you can gain a little percentage by cashing one of the top honours before crossing to dummy for the first finesse. You will lose out in the 2% event that East has all five missing cards, but you will gain in the 2.8% case where West has a singleton queen. An advantage of less than 1% may seem hardly worth bothering about, but if you can consistently muster such small extra chances in your favour you will be a big winner in the long run.

Bring one of the small cards from dummy into the South hand and the situation changes.

.6 4

A K J 10 9 3

Now the best chance is the 48% shot of leading twice from dummy for a finesse. When the finesse is right you will lose a trick only if West is void. It is true that you can cater for a singleton queen in the West hand by cashing a top honour first, but if you do that you will lose when West has a *small* singleton, which is four times as probable as the singleton queen.

[35]

Here is another situation where the correct play depends on the number of tricks you need.

K J 5 4

A 6 3

Needing all four tricks, you start with the ace and continue with a finesse of the jack, but the probability of success is no better than 18%, since you need to find a 3–3 break and the queen with West. Still, there is a 69% chance of making at least three tricks by this method.

Again you can increase the chance of making three tricks by abandoning the attempt to make four. Cash the king and ace of the suit, then lead from hand towards the jack. This caters for the possibility that East has the doubleton queen, boosting the chance of making three tricks to 77%.

The odds are not so generous with the next combination.

J 5 4

A K 6 3

Here the best you can do is cash one top honour and then lead low towards the jack. You will make three tricks when the queen is with West and also when East has Q x x or Q singleton, a total chance of 69%. The alternative of playing ace, king and another is about 15% worse.

When both the queen and the jack are missing the position may be finely balanced.

6 3

A K 10 9 2

Suppose that you need four tricks and have plenty of entries in both hands. There are two reasonable methods of approach. You may start by cashing the ace and king, continuing with the ten.

This method succeeds when the suit breaks 3–3 and also when either opponent has a doubleton honour.

Alternatively, you may lead twice from dummy and take two finesses. This method gives a slightly improved chance of making four tricks. Finessing twice loses when West has Q J x (7.1%) or Q J doubleton (1.6%), but gains when West has a small doubleton (9.7%), giving this line a 1% edge over starting with the ace and king. The overall chance of success is nearly 66%.

The next arrangement looks similar but requires a different approach.

K 3

A 10 9 6 2

Again you need four tricks, and both opponents follow with low cards to the play of the king. East plays another low card when you continue with the three. Should you finesse the nine or play the ace?

Both plays work when the suit breaks 3–3, and neither play succeeds when West has four cards or East has five. The only relevant situation, in fact, is where West has a doubleton. There are fifteen possible doubleton combinations, one of which (QJ) is already ruled out. If you take the trouble to set out the remaining fourteen, you will see that eight of them contain an honour card and six do not.* The percentage play, therefore, is to put up the ace on the second round. This has an edge of about 3% over taking the finesse.

Let's try one of the intermediate cards in dummy instead of the three.

K 9

A 10 6 3 2

* Just as we might expect, since six is $_4C_2$—the number of ways the four small cards can be combined two at a time.

Prospects are now less rosy, but by far the best way of trying for four tricks is to lead low from hand for a finesse of the nine. You will succeed when the suit breaks 3–3, when either opponent has Q J doubleton, when West has a doubleton honour and when West has Q J x x, giving a total chance of 61%.

Move the three back to dummy and we have another new situation.

K 9 3

A 10 6 2

This time your aim is to make three tricks, and there are three reasonable ways of going about it. If you start by cashing the top honours you will have a 70% chance of success. Slightly better is to lead low to the king and return the three for a finesse of the ten, which gives you a 72% chance. But the best odds, in fact, come from leading a low card for a first-round finesse of dummy's nine. If this loses, you continue by cashing the king and then, unless West shows out, the ace. This line of play offers a 75% chance of making three tricks. See if you can arrive at these percentage figures yourself by setting out the various distributions against which each line of play succeeds. It's a useful exercise.

6 5

A Q 10 9 3

With this holding the percentage play is to lead twice from dummy, finessing the nine and then the ten. This gives you a 59% chance of making four tricks, and a 9% of making all five (when East has K J or K J x).

The situation changes when it is possible to take only one finesse.

5

A Q 10 9 6 3

If you can afford to lose only one trick the best shot is to finesse the queen. You will succeed when the suit breaks 3–3 and the king is with East, also when East has the doubleton king and when either opponent has the doubleton jack, giving a total chance of 40%. Finessing the nine or ten is over 6% worse, for it loses not to four of the doubleton honour combinations but to eight (when West has either K x or J x).

A 6

J 10 5 4 2

Suppose you need to make three tricks with this combination. Obviously you will have no problem when the suit breaks 3–3 and no chance when it breaks 5–1 or 6–0. It is the 4–2 divisions that are crucial. The percentage play is to lead low to the ace and, no matter what East plays on the next round, play low again from hand. This caters for a doubleton honour (more probable than a small doubleton, as we have seen) in the West hand, and gives a 65% chance of success.

An interesting defensive point arises. Clearly if East has something like K Q 8 3 he should not rush up with the king or queen on the second round but calmly play low, hoping that declarer knows his percentage plays.

Many would echo the declarer's mistake on this hand.

```
                      ♠ 6
                      ♡ K 10 3
                      ◇ A 8 6 5 2
                      ♣ K J 7 5

   ♠ Q 8                  N           ♠ K 9 7 2
   ♡ 8 7 4 2          W       E       ♡ A 6
   ◇ K Q J 9              S           ◇ 10 7 3
   ♣ 10 6 3                           ♣ Q 9 4 2

                      ♠ A J 10 5 4 3    S       N
  Game all.           ♡ Q J 9 5        1 S     2 D
  Dealer South.       ◇ 4              2 H     2 NT
                      ♣ A 8            4 S      —
```

West led the king of diamonds to dummy's ace, and South immediately led a trump for a finesse of the ten. That was the end of the story, for the defenders could not be prevented from making three trump tricks and the ace of hearts.

South could afford only two trump losers and the situation was similar to that of our previous example. Again it boils down to a comparison between the probability of a doubleton honour in the West hand and that of a small doubleton. Since the former is more likely, South should have played the ace of spades at trick two and continued with a low spade from hand. The difference between the two lines of play is only about 3%, but that is often enough to tip the balance between success and failure.

Here is a further situation where the correct play depends on the number of tricks you can afford to lose.

3

K Q 8 7 6 4 2

If you can afford to lose only one trick, naturally you must lead from dummy and play an honour, hoping to find East with the ace doubleton. The probability of success is a slender $13\frac{1}{2}\%$, although your chance of making five tricks by this method is over 70%.

As usual, you can increase your chance of making five tricks by giving up the attempt to make six. Play a low card from both hands on the first round. This caters for the possibility of a singleton ace with West, giving you almost 3% extra.

Here is a combination that is often bothersome.

A 8 7 2

Q 10 9 4

If you need three tricks from the suit, the best chance is to take two finesses, leading the ten and running it if West plays low, and subsequently running the nine. You will fail only when East has K J, K J x or K J x x, giving you a 78% chance of success. Note that it is inferior by 2% to lead the queen for the first finesse, since this loses when East has all five missing cards.

The trouble with the alternative line of playing the ace first is that you will lose not only when West has K J x, K J x x or K J x x x, but sometimes when West has K x or J x as well, for you will have to guess when East plays low on the second round.

4

Combining Chances

In the last chapter we examined some familiar combinations of cards and practised working out the probabilities of various lines of play within a single suit. Now we are going to consider complete deals and look at ways of combining chances in more than one suit. First we must establish some ground rules for compounding probabilities.

♠ J 10 8 7 5
♡ K 4 2
◇ A Q 4 3
♣ A

♠ A Q 6 4 2
♡ A 9 5
◇ K 7 6
♣ 8 6

There are two different situations, both of which can be illustrated by the following example.

Suppose that you play in a sensible contract of six spades and receive a club lead. You need either a successful trump finesse (a 50% chance), or alternatively a 3–3 diamond break (a 36% chance) to enable you to dispose of your heart loser. But it would be wrong to conclude that your probability of success is therefore 86%. That would be to count some of your chances twice—those cases where both the spades and the diamonds behave kindly. It is only when the spade finesse fails that the diamond break comes into the picture.

Naturally you finesse in trumps at trick two. Out of 100 times when this situation occurs, the finesse succeeds in 50, and in these cases you make your slam irrespective of what happens in diamonds. In the other 50 cases where the finesse loses you have to fall back on the 36% chance of the diamond break, succeeding in a further 18 cases. The overall success rate for the contract is therefore 68%.

We can formulate a general rule for this situation, where you need only one out of two favourable outcomes and you can arrange the play so that the failure of the first event does not prejudice your chance of trying the other. The overall chance of success is obtained by adding the probability of the first event to the product of the probability of the second event and the failure zone of the first.

The law governing the situation can be written in mathematical form as follows:

$$P_{A \cup B} = P_A + (1 - P_A) . P_B$$

P_A stands for the probability that the event A will occur. It has to be expressed as a decimal or a percentage. The expression $A \cup B$, called "A or B" or "the union of A and B", is the event that at least one of A and B occurs.

Now suppose that on the same hand, pressing for points, you arrive in a bold, bad contract of seven spades. This time you require both the spade finesse and the diamond break. You are down straight away on the 50 occasions when the trump finesse loses. If the trump finesse wins, you are still dependent on the 3–3 diamond break, which will occur in 36% of the remaining 50 occasions—i.e. 18 times. The success rate for the grand slam is therefore 18%.

In this second situation, where you require two favourable events, the probability of success is obtained by multiplying the probabilities of the two separate events. In mathematical notation:

$$P_{A \cap B} = P_A . P_B$$

The expression $A \cap B$, called "A and B" or "the intersection of A and B", is the event that both A and B occur.

In using these formulae, we generally assume that P_A and P_B, the probabilities of the events A and B, are known at the start, and that P_B does not depend on the outcome of A. Often this is correct, as in the example we have just considered, where the location of the king of spades does not influence the chance of a 3–3 diamond break. In other cases there will be some small change in P_B but not enough to be worth worrying about in a practical calculation.

For example, consider the common situation where you need one out of two finesses for your contract. Our formula gives the probability of success as $50\% + (1 - 50\%).50\% = 75\%$. This is an approximate answer, because the outcome of one finesse does have a slight effect on the chances of the other. More precisely, the probability of success is 76% if the two finesses are taken into the same defender's hand and 74% if the finesses are taken into opposite hands.

We can see this if we reflect that one of two finesses into the same hand will succeed whenever the two key cards are divided (52%) and half the time when they are together (24%)—a total chance of 76%. Finessing into opposite hands, you will succeed whenever the key cards are together (48%) and half the time when they are split (26%)—a total chance of 74%.

There are times when the odds will change considerably as the hand develops, and we shall examine such cases systematically in later chapters.

Meanwhile let us see some more examples.

♠ J 4
♡ 8 7 4 2
◇ A 7 3
♣ A K 8 2

♠ A 3
♡ A Q
◇ K 9 8 5 2
♣ Q 6 5 4

The contact is three no trumps and West leads the six of spades to the jack, queen and ace.

There are only seven top tricks and you lack the tempo to develop the diamonds. You must therefore hope to find the clubs 3–2 and the heart finesse right. You need two favourable events, in fact, and the probability of success is the product of the probabilities of the 3–2 club break and the heart finesse—68% × 50% = 34%.

Now let us strengthen the hands a little. The contract is the same, and so is the play to the first trick.

This time you can make do with *either* the club break *or* the heart finesse. You can test the clubs first, and if they fail to break 3–2 you will still be in a position to take two heart finesses.

The probability of success is therefore obtained by adding the probability of the 3–2 club break to the product of the probability of the heart finesse and the failure zone of the 3–2 club break. The calculation is as follows:

♠ J 4
♡ 8 7 4
◇ A 7 3
♣ A K 8 5 2

♠ A 3
♡ A Q J
◇ K 9 8 5 2
♣ Q 6 4

Clubs 3–2	68%
Clubs 4–1 or worse but heart finesse right $(1 - 68\%) 50\% = 32\% \times 50\%$	16%
Total	**84%**

It is easy to overlook the possibility of combining chances.

♠ 7 5
♡ 3
◇ 8 6 5 4
♣ K Q 8 7 4 3

♠ A K 4
♡ A 10 9 6 2
◇ A K 3
♣ A 5

Again the contract is three no trumps, and West leads the jack of spades to your king.

There are eight tricks on top, and the odds are better than two to one that you will make three extra tricks in clubs.

But it would be foolish to rely entirely on the 68% chance of a 3–2 club break, for the extra trick you need may be available in diamonds. The correct play at trick two is to lead the diamond three from hand. You can win any return, cash the top diamonds and then test the clubs, with the following chances for your contract.

Diamonds 3–3	36%
Diamonds 4–2 or worse but clubs 3–2	
(1 − 36%) 68% = 64% × 68%	44%
Total	80%

The order of playing the suits cannot be reversed, for if the clubs are tackled first the chance of establishing an extra diamond trick is lost for lack of an entry. Note that the play of a low diamond at trick two brings in twelve tricks when both suits break kindly.

The next example is more complex.

West leads the five of hearts against three no trumps and dummy's king wins the trick.

You have six top tricks, the defenders are going to establish a seventh for you in hearts, and there is a good chance of finding the two extra tricks you need in the club suit.

Suppose you start with a club to the king and club back to the ace. If the clubs fail to break 3–2 you will not be completely bereft of hope. You can switch to spades in the hope of finding East with K Q x or a singleton or doubleton honour.

♠ J 7 4 3
♡ K J
◇ 10 4
♣ A Q 7 6 2

♠ A 10 9
♡ Q 8 3
◇ A J 5 2
♣ K 5 4

This will give extra chances of about 7% to add to your 68% for the 3–2 club break, giving an overall chance of 75%.

However, it is much better to lead a spade for a finesse of the nine at trick two. On regaining the lead you will cash the king and ace of clubs and, if the clubs break badly, finesse again in spades. This line of play will produce three spade tricks:

Whenever East has both spade honours	24%
When East has K x or Q x (8 × 1.61%)	13%
When East has K x x or Q x x (12 × 1.78%)	21%
When East has K or Q bare (2 × 1.21%)	2%
	60%

Multiplying this figure by the failure zone of the 3–2 club break (32%), we get an extra 19% to add to our 68%, giving us a total chance of 87%.

This is not the sort of calculation that can be made at the table, and it is set out here just to show how it is done. Nevertheless, an experienced declarer should realise intuitively that the odds favour playing on spades before touching clubs.

There may be finessing possibilities in more than one suit.

♠ Q 10 4 3
♡ 9 7 4
◇ 10 3
♣ A J 8 2

♠ A K J 9 5
♡ 6
◇ A K J 9
♣ K 10 5

You arrive in six spades and West leads the queen of hearts. East encourages and West continues with a second heart for you to ruff. When you test the trumps they prove to be 2–2. How should you continue?

A successful finesse in clubs would solve all your problems. Less obviously, a first-round diamond finesse might do as well, for after finessing twice in diamonds you would be able to discard dummy's club losers. There is no possibility of combining these finessing plays, but there is always the chance of dropping a singleton or doubleton queen in one of the suits.

You could start by cashing the ace and king of diamonds, for instance, and then, if the queen did not appear, try to guess the clubs. Alternatively, you could start with the top clubs and then, if there is no joy, run the ten of diamonds.

The question of which suit to tackle first is answered by considering which queen is more likely to drop. *The rule in these situations is to cash the tops in the longer suit, then finesse in the shorter.* A glance at the table on page 23 will confirm that the frequency of a singleton or doubleton queen is significantly greater when the opponents have six cards than when they have seven. You should therefore play the king and ace of clubs, and then run the ten of diamonds if the club queen has not appeared. The probability of success for this line is:

Club queen singleton or doubleton	19%
Diamond finesse right (81% × 50%)	40%
Total	59%

Obviously this line of play risks a two-trick defeat, but extra undertricks are of little moment when you are trying for a slam.

Tackling the suits the other way round gives a reduced chance of success.

Diamond queen singleton or doubleton	10%
Second-round club finesse (90% × 51%)	46%
Total	56%

On certain hands it is possible to combine chances in three suits. The formulae on pages 43 and 44 can be extended to cover such cases in the obvious way, by first working out the probability for the union or the intersection of two of the chances, and then treating this combined event as A and the third as B.

The contract is three no trumps, and in spite of your 29 high-card points you cannot be certain of success when West leads the jack of hearts to your ace.

♠ K 7 6 4
♡ 8 3
◇ K 8 6 3
♣ A 5 2

Still, there are a number of chances, any one of which will give you the contract. The spades may break 3–3, one of the minor-suit finesses may be right, and there is always the possibility of dropping a minor-suit queen.

♠ A Q 5
♡ A 6
◇ A J 7 2
♣ K J 8 3

As always, if you are going to play for the drop in one suit and finesse in the other, it is in the longer suit (diamonds in this case) that you should play for the drop. The order of play is therefore three rounds of spades followed by the ace and king of diamonds. If nothing favourable happens, take your last chance with a second-round finesse in clubs. A rough calculation gives the following figures:

Spades 3–3	36%
Queen of diamonds drops (64% × 33%)	21%
Second-round club finesse (43% × 51%)	22%
Total	79%

Note that the 51% for the club finesse has to be multiplied by the failure zone of the other two chances.

On this hand your remaining chances are not prejudiced by the failure of either of the first two steps, so you could equally well reverse the order of play, trying to drop the queen of diamonds before testing the spades. This does not affect the odds in any way. The calculation simply becomes:

Queen of diamonds drops	33%
Spades 3–3 (67% × 36%)	24%
Second-round club finesse (43% × 51%)	22%
Total	79%

The principle of trying to drop an honour in one suit before finessing in another holds good even when the missing honour is the king.

♠ 7 6
♡ K Q 10 6 3
♢ 4
♣ A Q J 8 5

♠ A 9
♡ A J 9 8 2
♢ A Q 5
♣ 10 4 3

You are in six hearts, and West hits your weak spot with a lead of the queen of spades. After winning the spade ace and drawing trumps in two rounds, you have to decide on the best play.

The choice lies between finessing in clubs, which is likely to produce thirteen tricks if West has the king, and taking a diamond finesse in the hope of discarding dummy's losing spade on the ace of diamonds. In fact the diamond finesse is the better shot, because you can first take the opportunity of trying to drop a singleton club king. Your chances are:

Club king singleton	6%
Diamond finesse (94% × 50%)	47%
Total	53%

Again you risk going two down for the sake of an increased chance of landing the slam.

Note that a declarer who opts for the club finesse can boost his chances slightly by first cashing the diamond ace and then ruffing the small diamond in dummy. If the king drops, he can return to hand with a trump and discard dummy's spade on the diamond queen. When the opponents hold nine cards, however, the chance of finding a singleton or doubleton honour is pretty slender. The calculation is:

Diamond king singleton or doubleton	2%
Club finesse (98% × 50%)	49%
Total	51%

So far the best odds have come from combining chances in as many suits as possible, but this is not always the case.

West leads a passive trump against your contract of six diamonds. You draw the outstanding trumps in three rounds, discarding a spade and a heart from the table. How should you continue?

♠ 8 4
♡ A 9 7 6 2
◇ 4
♣ K Q 10 5 3

There are eleven top tricks and chances for the twelfth in three suits. It might seem a good idea to start with the heart suit, ruffing the third round. If the hearts failed to break, you would still have the chance of 3–3 clubs or the club jack dropping. And if all else failed you could fall back on a lead towards the king of spades. Let's calculate the chances for this line of play.

| N |
| W E |
| S |

♠ K 7 6
♡ K 3
◇ A K Q J 9 5
♣ A 6

Hearts 3–3	36%
Clubs 3–3 or club jack drops (64% × 54%)	35%
Spade ace with East (29% × 50%)	14%
	—
Total	85%

That's not at all bad, but in fact you can do better by abandoning the heart suit and concentrating on clubs. Relegating the heart ace to the role of entry card gives additional chances in the club suit that more than compensate for the loss of the 3–3 heart split. Now you will succeed when the clubs break 3–3 *or* 4–2, and also when the club jack is bare. Your chances are:

Clubs 3–3 or 4–2 or club jack bare	86%
Spade ace with East (14% × 50%)	7%
	—
Total	93%

The odds may favour concentrating entirely on one suit.

♠ 8 5
♡ 9 5 4
◇ A Q 8 7 2
♣ J 8 3

♠ A K Q 4
♡ A 7 3
◇ K 6
♣ A 10 9 4

West leads the queen of hearts against your contract of three no trumps. You play low, and West continues with a small heart to his partner's king. Again you hold off, and East perseveres with a third heart, West following with the ten.

You have eight top tricks and chances of a ninth in either diamonds or clubs. It seems natural to start with three rounds of diamonds, discarding the low spade from hand. If diamonds fail to break 3–3 you can switch to clubs, and you will succeed when East has both club honours, or a singleton or doubleton club honour with the long diamonds. This combination play gives an overall chance of about 56%.

The club suit on its own offers better odds, however. If you can make three clubs you need only two tricks from diamonds. The correct play, therefore, is to overtake the king of diamonds with the ace and run the club eight. On regaining the lead you can cross to the queen of diamonds and run the club jack, and you will make the contract whenever East has at least one club honour—76% of the time.

Overtaking plays can often augment your chances when entries are short in one hand or the other.

The contract is again three no trumps, and West leads the jack of hearts to your king.

You could unblock the king and queen of clubs and continue with a low diamond from hand. If the clubs failed to break you would later be able to take a diamond finesse, which gives you 68% plus roughly half of the failure zone for a total chance of 84%.

However, when clubs are 3–2 you can afford to give up a club trick on this hand, so you may as well award yourself an extra entry to dummy by overtaking with the ace of clubs on

♠ J 4
♡ A 3
◇ 9 7 3
♣ A 8 6 5 4 3

♠ A 10 6
♡ K 7 5
◇ A Q 10 8 2
♣ K Q

the second round. If both opponents follow, you simply concede a club. And if the clubs prove to be 4–1 or 5–0, you take advantage of your additional entry by running the seven of diamonds. This line succeeds when the clubs are 3–2 (68%) and also when East has at least one of the diamond honours ($32\% \times 76\% = 24\%$), giving you a total chance of 92%.

There are certain hands on which the best line of play is not immediately obvious.

♠ A 8 5
♡ Q 7 2
♢ J 6 2
♣ A 7 6 4

♠ K 7
♡ A J 4
♢ A Q 10 9 5 4
♣ K Q

West leads the jack of spades against your contract of six no trumps. How do you plan the play?

A straightforward plan would be to win with the ace of spades and run the jack of diamonds. You would succeed whenever East held the king of diamonds, and if West held the king you would still have the chance of finding the diamonds 2–2, in which case, after unblocking the clubs, you could use the six of diamonds as an entry for the heart finesse. The chances can be summarized as follows:

Diamond king with East	50%
Diamond king with West (50%) but diamonds 2–2 ($\times$ 40%) and heart finesse right ($\times$ 50%)	10%
Total	60%

You might think of winning the first trick in hand and cashing the ace of diamonds at trick two, but this is no improvement. It succeeds only when the diamond king is bare (about 12%) or when the heart finesse is right ($88\% \times 50\%$), a total expectancy of 56%.

The best shot is to win the opening lead with the ace of spades and lead a heart for a finesse of the jack. If this loses to the king, the queen of hearts and the ace of clubs supply the two entries that you may need for diamond finesses. If the jack of hearts wins at trick two you are practically home, for you can now play the queen of diamonds from hand. When both opponents follow suit but the king does not appear, you can unblock the clubs and continue with the ten of diamonds, forcing the defenders to allow you access to dummy with the jack of diamonds for a discard of your losing heart on the club ace.

If West shows out on the first round of diamonds there is no problem. East may refuse to win, but in that case you simply overtake a club in dummy and pick up the diamond king by finessing. You are not without hope even if it is East who shows out on the first round of diamonds. After unblocking the clubs, you play a diamond to dummy's jack, discard your small heart on the ace of clubs, and revert to diamonds. West will be able to defeat you only if he began with four or more clubs.

The overall chances for this line of play are calculated as follows:

Heart jack loses (50%) but diamond finesse right (× 50%)	25%
Heart jack wins (50%) and West does not have all four diamonds with four or more clubs (× 98%)	49%
Total	74%

5

The Care of Options

As declarer, you will naturally attempt to stack the odds in your favour by testing several possibilities before committing yourself to one particular line of play. Given freedom of manoeuvre, you may be able to take advantage of all the available options, arranging your plays in such a way that failure at any stage but the final one will not result in immediate defeat.

But freedom of manoeuvre cannot be taken for granted. If the lead has to be surrendered, the defenders will be quick to attack your options, forcing you to make a decision in a critical suit before you are ready to commit yourself. The defenders have an advantage in that they know how your suits are breaking long before you do. If a side suit is breaking well and a finesse is wrong, they will offer you the finesse at the first opportunity. They will do the same when the suit is breaking badly and the finesse is right, and you will be bound to make the wrong decision some of the time. For practical players, any calculation of probabilities must take account of this factor.

Your aim must be to avoid, whenever possible, having to make an embarrassing premature commitment. Often the dilemma can be circumvented by testing the side suit first. Alternatively, an avoidance play of some sort may ensure that a dangerous opponent cannot gain the lead at an early stage.

Even when there is no question of a damaging lead from a defender, it can be easy to lose an option through carelessness. The order in which you test your suits can make a significant difference to your probability of success. There are certain hands on which you do not know how many losers you can afford in one suit until you discover how another suit behaves.

Here is an example.

♠ 8 6 5
♡ 9 4 2
◇ A K 8 3
♣ A 6 3

♠ A Q 7 4 3 2
♡ A Q
◇ 7 2
♣ 10 8 4

West leads the jack of diamonds against your contract of four spades. You win with the ace and East plays the six. How should you continue?

It's no great contract, for there are two certain club losers and potential losers in both major suits. The trumps can be brought in without loss only when East has K x, but if you take a first-round finesse you run the risk of losing to a singleton king.

The safety play to guard against this possibility is to play the ace of trumps on the first round. This gives the maximum chance of holding your trump losers to one trick. Should you play a trump to the ace at trick two?

That would be unwise, for at the moment you do not know if you can afford even one loser in trumps. You cannot tell until you discover whether or not you have a heart loser. That is the key to the problem. To give yourself the best chance you must lead a heart for a finesse of the queen at trick two.

If the heart finesse succeeds you can afford to safety-play the spades, cashing the ace, crossing to the king of diamonds and playing another spade towards the queen. You will make the contract when the spades are 2–2, and also in five of the eight 3–1 combinations. If the heart finesse fails, you must try to avoid a spade loser by finessing the queen on the first round. The overall chance of success is calculated as follows:

Heart finesse right (50%) and East has two or three
spades or bare king (40.7% + 31.1%)   36%
Heart finesse wrong (50%) but East has K x in spades
(20.3%)   10%
                                            _____
                                    Total   46%

Taking the spade finesse at trick two reduces your chance of success by over 3%.

The more dangerous situations are those where a defender may launch a damaging attack on your options.

West leads the six of spades against your contract of three no trumps and East plays the two. How do you plan the play?

♠ J 10
♡ A Q 3
◇ Q 10 6 3
♣ Q J 7 2

Clearly a successful club finesse is all that you need for game. Failing that, you have the chance of making four diamond tricks with the heart finesse in reserve.

♠ K 9 4
♡ 9 8 6
◇ A K 5
♣ A 10 9 4

Since the club finesse can be taken into the "safe" hand, it may seem natural to run the queen of clubs at trick two. But you have to think about what will happen if the finesse loses. Any reasonable bridge player in the West seat will switch to a heart, whether he has the king or not. This will force you to make a premature choice between your two remaining options. If you go up with the ace of hearts and play on diamonds, you may end up a trick short and discover, to your chagrin, that the heart finesse was right all the time. At best, your chances are 50% for the club finesse plus 30% (50% × 60%) in the diamond suit—a total of 80%.

[57]

How much better to enjoy all your options by testing the diamonds first. After three rounds of diamonds you run the queen of clubs as before. The difference is that if the finesse loses and a heart comes back, you know what you need from hearts. If the diamonds have produced four tricks, you go up with the ace of hearts and claim your contract. If the diamonds have yielded only three tricks, you have to risk the heart finesse. Your probability of success is:

Diamond jack drops or East has singleton or void	60%
Club finesse wins (40% × 50%)	20%
Heart finesse wins (20% × 50%)	10%
Total	90%

The problem is similar on the next hand and so is the solution.

♠ Q 10 9 3
♡ A 8
◇ J 7 5
♣ A Q 6 4

```
      N
  W       E
      S
```

♠ K J
♡ 9 7 5 3
◇ A Q 4
♣ K 8 5 2

West leads the four of hearts against your contract of three no trumps. Since he is not likely to have underled three honours, it seems a good idea to attempt to block the suit. When you play the ace of hearts East follows with the ten. What now?

You can establish three tricks in spades which, with four clubs and two aces, will be enough for game. The trouble is you can't be sure of making four club tricks.

Suppose you start on the spades and someone takes the ace. East will win the heart continuation and place you on the guessing griddle by returning a diamond. Naturally you will prefer the 68% chance of the 3–2 club break to the 50–50 shot of the finesse, but you will have lost a valuable option unnecessarily.

Once again the right move is to test the side suit first, playing a low club to your king and a club back to the queen. If both defenders follow suit you can safely switch to spades. But if someone shows out on the second club you will have to risk the diamond finesse, and you should lead a diamond to your queen at trick four. Playing diamonds before spades will gain when West has the diamond king and East the spade ace. If West began with five hearts, as seems likely, he will be unable to regain the lead after the hearts have been unblocked.

On the assumption that the hearts are 5–2, we can calculate roughly as follows:

Clubs 3–2	68%
Diamond finesse right (32% × 50%)	16%
Diamond finesse wrong but East has ♠A (16% × 50%)	8%
Total	92%

To determine the right way of taking a finesse it is often necessary to ask yourself which of the defenders is in a position to damage your options.

The contract is six diamonds and West leads the jack of clubs to your ace. Trumps are drawn, East discarding a spade on the second round. How should you proceed?

Obviously you must tackle hearts before spades, for the spade finesse will be unnecessary if the hearts' are 3–3. A successful finesse of the queen of hearts would allow you to test the heart division before committing yourself in spades. But there is the usual problem. If the finesse of the queen of hearts loses, a spade will come back and one of your options will disappear. You will have to make an immediate choice between finessing in spades and playing for a 3–3 heart split, and your overall chance will be no better than 62%.

♠ 7 6
♡ A Q 6 4
◇ J 10 6 3
♣ K 8 5

```
        N
    W       E
        S
```

♠ A Q
♡ J 8 3
◇ A K Q 9 5 4
♣ A 4

[59]

You can do much better by crossing to dummy and leading a low heart towards your jack. This line will succeed whenever the hearts are 3–3 and also when East has the king singleton or doubleton. You cannot be forced to take a view in spades before you know if the hearts are breaking, and your probability of success rises to 74%.

But on this hand you can increase your chances still further by playing on elimination lines. Play a club to the king, ruff the third club, cross to the ace of hearts and return a low heart from dummy. Now you will succeed whenever the king of hearts comes down in three rounds (54%) and also when the spade finesse is right (46% × 50%), giving you a total chance of 77%.

At times it is right to reject a finesse altogether in order to avoid compromising an option.

♠ A J 9 5 3
♡ 5
♢ J 6
♣ K Q 7 6 3

♠ Q 10 8 6 4
♡ A 7
♢ A Q 7 3
♣ A 2

The contract is six spades and West leads the queen of hearts to your ace.

By now the problem is familiar. The normal percentage play in spades is to take the finesse, but a losing spade finesse will inevitably result in a diamond return. With no chance to test for a 3–3 club break, you will be reduced to relying on one or two finesses—a 74% chance.

By accepting a diminished chance of catching the king of spades, you can increase the overall probability of success. The best play is to ruff the small heart at trick two and then cash the ace of spades. If the king drops, your troubles are over. If both defenders follow suit but the king does not fall, you play on clubs, discarding a diamond from your hand and ruffing the fourth round if necessary. When West has the king of spades you are home, for if he refuses to over-ruff a club you simply throw him in with a trump to make a fatal return. If East started with K x in trumps and the clubs are not 3–3, you still have the chance of the diamond finesse.

You also have considerable chances when the trumps are 3–0. If West has the trumps, you knock out the king and draw the third round before testing the clubs. If East has the trumps, you test the clubs before playing a second trump.

Your chances can be summarized as follows:

Spade king drops	26%
Spade K x with West	26%
Spade K x with East (26%) but clubs 3–3 or diamond finesse right (36% + (64% × 50%))	18%
Spade K x x with West (11%) but clubs 3–3 or diamond finesse right (36% + (64% × 50%))	$7\frac{1}{2}$%
Spade K x x with East (11%) but clubs 3–3 or no worse than 4–2 with diamonds right (36% + (48% × 50%))	$6\frac{1}{2}$%
Total	84%

There is a pleasing paradox about the situation, for if the trump finesse is working there is no need to take it. This is often the case on those hands where elimination technique can add to your chances. Here is a further example.

West leads a spade against your contract of six clubs. If you put up the ace and take an immediate club finesse, a diamond is likely to come back, robbing you of one of your options. Again you will be reduced to the 74% chance of banking on one of two finesses.

♠ A 5 4
♡ K Q 7 3
◇ A 7 4
♣ 9 5 3

As in the last hand, the right shot is to reject the trump finesse. If East has the king of clubs you are virtually certain to make the slam anyway. Ruff the opening lead and cash the ace of clubs. If both defenders follow with small cards, play a heart to the queen, cash the ace of spades for a diamond

♠ —
♡ A 8 4
◇ Q J 9
♣ A Q J 7 6 4 2

discard and ruff the third spade. Now play the ace of hearts and a heart to the king. If the suit does not break 3–3, ruff the fourth heart and exit with a trump. If East has to win, your troubles are over. And if West wins you can still fall back on the diamond finesse.

Naturally, if the king of clubs drops under the ace you will draw the outstanding trump before trying for the overtrick. And if the trumps are 3–0, you will continue with the queen of clubs to force out the king. This time the total probability of success falls just short of 83%. Check it for yourself.

It may be argued that if you take a losing trump finesse at trick two there is no certainty that a diamond will be returned. That is true, although a competent defender in the West seat should see the advantage of attacking an option. But if you allow that a diamond will come back just half the time, the play of the ace of clubs at trick two still beats the finesse by a clear 3%.

The neglect of a small precaution cost the declarer an option on the next hand.

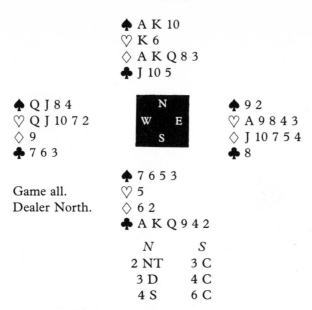

♠ A K 10
♡ K 6
◇ A K Q 8 3
♣ J 10 5

♠ Q J 8 4
♡ Q J 10 7 2
◇ 9
♣ 7 6 3

♠ 9 2
♡ A 9 8 4 3
◇ J 10 7 5 4
♣ 8

♠ 7 6 5 3
♡ 5
◇ 6 2
♣ A K Q 9 4 2

Game all.
Dealer North.

N	S
2 NT	3 C
3 D	4 C
4 S	6 C

West led the queen of hearts which was allowed to win the first trick. Realising that there could hardly be a second heart trick for the defence, and seeing little hope unless East had the diamonds well stopped, West made a far-sighted switch to the eight of spades.

Declarer counted eleven top tricks and worked out that he had an 84% chance of establishing a twelfth trick in diamonds. He naturally rejected the 24% chance of the double spade finesse, putting up the ace, drawing trumps and playing on diamonds. Had the suit broken no worse than 4–2 he would have been successful, but on the 5–1 diamond break the slam had to go one down.

The diamond break was unlucky, but declarer could have protected himself against the attack on the spade option by covering the queen of hearts at trick one. East cannot profitably attack spades from his side of the table, and later, when the 5–1 diamond split comes to light, South can try the deep finesse in spades. The extra 4% (16% × 24%) chance comes off in this case.

Instead of offering you an immediate finesse, the defenders may attack an option by forcing you to make a premature discard.

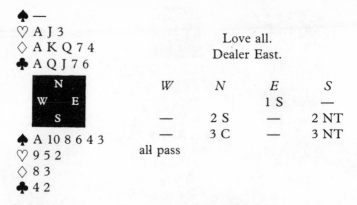

♠ —
♡ A J 3
◇ A K Q 7 4
♣ A Q J 7 6

Love all.
Dealer East.

♠ A 10 8 6 4 3
♡ 9 5 2
◇ 8 3
♣ 4 2

W	N	E	S
		1 S	—
—	2 S	—	2 NT
—	3 C	—	3 NT
all pass			

West leads the nine of spades against your contract of three no trumps. You throw the three of hearts from dummy, East puts in the jack and you win the ace. How should you continue?

There are six top tricks, a seventh can be developed in clubs, and it looks as though the contract will be made when either minor suit breaks 3–3, making you the favourite at 3 to 2 on.

But a certain amount of care is required. Although you cannot expect the club finesse to be right, it may seem harmless enough to take a losing club finesse at trick two. In fact it is far from harmless. After winning the king of clubs East will continue with the king and queen of spades, forcing two discards from the table. You can spare the jack of hearts, but on the third spade you have to shorten one of the minor suits. If you make the wrong choice, discarding from the suit that is breaking 3–3, you can wave the game goodbye. In taking the club finesse you manage at a stroke to reduce your chances from 60% to 36%.

On this hand the first priority must be given to finding out how

[64]

the diamonds are breaking. After winning the first trick you should play the ace and king of diamonds and, if nobody shows out, continue with the queen. If the diamonds do not split evenly, you still have time to switch to clubs and try for a 3–3 break there.

This hand emphasises once again the importance of testing the break in a side suit at the earliest opportunity. There are, of course, other ways in which an extra option may be preserved. One of these combines the elements of avoidance and elimination play.

West leads the ten of spades against your contract of six hearts. Both opponents follow suit when you play a trump to your ace. What now?

♠ K
♡ Q J 7 3
◇ J 8 6 5 4
♣ K 8 4

♠ A 6 5
♡ A K 10 8 5 2
◇ A Q
♣ Q 6

It is time to take stock. If you draw the outstanding trump at this point you will be left with nothing but the 50% chance of the diamond finesse, and it would be a pity to waste the intriguing possibilities in the club suit. If you could manage to slip past the ace of clubs, you could discard a club from dummy on the ace of spades and eventually hope to throw in the defender who has the club ace. There would be no point in throwing in East, so you must play West for the ace of clubs.

Lead the six of clubs from hand at trick three. If West has the ace he cannot afford to take it immediately, for that establishes an eventual discard for your queen of diamonds. If dummy's king of clubs holds, you can return to hand with a trump, cash the ace of spades for a club discard, ruff your third spade in dummy and exit in clubs. On lead with the ace, West will have to play a diamond or concede a ruff and discard.

Note that you cannot afford to draw the outstanding trump before making your avoidance play in clubs. If you did that, you could return to hand only with a third round of trumps, which would leave dummy with no trumps at the moment of throw-in.

Provided that the play is timed correctly, your probability of success is 74%, for you will make the slam whenever West has the ace of clubs and also when East has the king of diamonds.

In this final example an avoidance play is helpful in a different way.

♠ Q J 9 3
♡ K Q 10
◇ A 7 4
♣ 8 7 5

♠ K 4
♡ A J 9 7 5 3 2
◇ —
♣ A Q 4 2

West leads the queen of diamonds against your contract of six hearts. Assuming a 2–1 trump break, how do you plan the play?

There are just two chances for the contract. The ten of spades may drop or the club finesse may work. The problem is to combine these chances in the optimum way.

Suppose that you discard a club on the ace of diamonds, draw trumps in two rounds, and lead a spade to your king. If West has the ace, your options will remain intact. You will be able to test for the fall of the ten of spades before committing yourself in clubs. But if East has the ace of spades he will take it on the second round and return a club. Then, unless the ten of spades has already dropped, you will have to abandon one of your options. The total chance for this line of play is nearly 62%.

You can do significantly better by retaining the ace of diamonds as a threat in dummy. Ruff the first trick, cross to dummy with a trump, and lead a spade towards your king. If East has the ace he cannot afford to play it on the first round. When the king wins, you can play a second trump to dummy, discard your small spade on the ace of diamonds, and then run the queen of spades through East. The difference is that you cannot be forced to take a view in clubs before you know how the spades are behaving.

Allowing for the risk of a second-round spade ruff, this line of play still gives an overall chance of success of about 67%.

6

Changing Odds

The time has come to consider how the probabilities change during the play of the hand. We start with the *a priori* probabilities relating to the division of the opponents' cards—those calculated before the deal and set out in the table on page 20. Everything that happens during the play, every new piece of information that comes to light, has its effect in modifying these probabilities. Often the effect is so small as to be negligible for practical purposes, but on other occasions the odds may change appreciably.

Indeed, the odds may be influenced even before the start of the play by the opponents' bidding or lack of bidding. For instance, if you and dummy together have five small cards in a suit and neither opponent has bid, in spite of favourable opportunities, the probability of one opponent holding seven or eight cards in the suit is virtually zero.

In most cases where the odds change significantly during the play, we can keep track of things by extending our ideas. The fresh information that comes in enables us to eliminate certain distributions as impossible, and the ratios of the probabilities of the holdings that are still possible lead us to revised percentage figures. These new figures—calculated after something has happened—are known as *a posteriori* probabilities.

Suppose that this is one of your suits.

You play off the ace and king, both opponents following suit. For the moment let us assume you are up against expert defenders who will false-card at random, so that you can read nothing into the size of their cards. What is the chance that both remaining cards will fall under the queen?

A K Q 5 3

4 2

To arrive at the answer we have to examine the entry in the table on page 20 under "six cards outstanding". When both opponents follow to two rounds, the 6–0 and the 5–1 distributions can be ruled out, but nothing has happened to cause us to revise our estimate of the relative probabilities of 4–2 and 3–3. This is an example of the "deletion principle", which can be stated as follows. *When the opponents follow to the play of a suit with insignificant cards, the impossible distributions are deleted, and the probabilities of the remainder retain their relative magnitudes.*

In the present example only the 3–3 and 4–2 distributions remain undeleted, with odds in the ratio of 35.53 to 48.45, or precisely 11 to 15. The new percentage figures are 42.3% for the 3–3 break and 57.7% for 4–2. That's a significant increase in the probability of the 3–3 break, but it still can't compete with the fifty-fifty chance of a finesse.

♠ 7 4
♡ Q 7 5 4 3
♢ 9 8 3
♣ A Q 6

♠ A 6
♡ A K
♢ A K 6 4
♣ J 10 7 4 2

The contract is three no trumps and the defenders attack in spades. You take the ace of spades and cash the two top hearts, both defenders following suit.

The prospects of an even break in hearts have improved, but not enough to justify rejection of the club finesse. Your best bet is to run the jack of clubs at trick four.

Now let us turn to another situation which at first sight looks similar.

Again both defenders follow suit with insignificant cards when you cash the ace and the king. Is it again a 42.3% chance that the suit will break 3–3?

A K Q 10 3

4 2

Not so. The difference this time is that the jack is a significant card——significant in the sense that a defender would never play it unless forced to do so. In applying the "deletion principle" we have to rule out not only the 6–0 and 5–1 divisions but also those 4–2 divisions that contain a doubleton jack, i.e. one third of the 4–2 divisions. The 3–3 divisions retain their full weight because a defender would not make things easy for you by playing the jack on the first or second round from J x x. So we are left with odds for the 3–3 and the remaining 4–2 distributions in the ratio of 35.53 to 32.3, or 11 to 10. In percentage terms, the probability of the 3–3 break has risen to 52.4%.

♠ 7 4
♡ Q 10 5 4 3
◇ 9 8 3
♣ A Q 6

♠ A 6
♡ A K
◇ A K 6 4
♣ J 10 7 4 2

If we alter the last hand slightly by putting the ten of hearts in dummy, the club finesse is no longer the favourite.

West leads a spade against your three no trumps. You win and cash the two top hearts. Both defenders follow suit but the jack does not appear.

Now the best shot is a club to the ace. Quite apart from the chance of finding a singleton king of clubs, you have a 52.4% chance of dropping the jack of hearts.

The situation is similar when it is the queen or the king that is missing from your suit. Here is another three no trump hand.

♠ K 5
♡ A K
◇ K J 8 6 4 3
♣ J 9 2

♠ A 8 7 2
♡ 7 6 5 4
◇ A
♣ K 10 8 7

West leads a heart to dummy's king. Since you have six top tricks, a successful finesse against the queen of clubs would see you home. However, there are also some chances in the diamond suit, so you start with a diamond to your ace, return to the table with the king of spades, and cash the king of diamonds. Both defenders follow but the queen does not appear.

Here, once again, you have to delete not only the 6–0 and 5–1 distributions but also the 4–2 divisions where either opponent has a doubleton queen of diamonds, and again the chance of a 3–3 diamond split has risen to 52.4%. The play of a third diamond is therefore a better shot than running the nine of clubs.

Now try your hand at a slam.

West leads a low spade against your contract of six hearts. You capture East's jack, draw a round of trumps with the ace, play a club to dummy's ace and ruff a club high. Both defenders follow to the second club but the king does not appear. When you continue with a trump to dummy's king, West discards a spade.

Now you have reached the crossroads. You can either lead a diamond towards your king, hoping to find the ace well-placed, or you can play for a 3–3 club break by ruffing

♠ 8 7
♡ K 10 2
◇ 7 4
♣ A Q 8 6 5 4

♠ A K
♡ A Q J 9 6 5 3
◇ K 8 5
♣ 3

another club. The club is in fact the better play since the probability of the 3–3 break has again risen to over 52%.

The odds change by exactly the same amount whether there is one significant card missing or two. Consider this common position.

A 10 9 8 3

K 2

Needing to develop tricks in this suit, you cash the king and continue with the two to dummy's ace (the percentage play, because a doubleton honour in the East hand is more probable than a small doubleton). As it happens, both defenders follow suit with small cards. Again we assume that you can read nothing into the order in which the small cards are played; the important thing is that a significant card—the queen or the jack—has not appeared. What is the probability that the suit will break 3–3?

Following the "deletion principle", we rule out all the 6–0 and 5–1 divisions. Also, since an honour card has not appeared, we can delete the 4–2 divisions that contain a doubleton honour (18 cases out of 30), and the 3–3 divisions where one defender has both honours (8 cases out of 20). We are left with odds in the ratio of $3/5 \times 35.53$ to $2/5 \times 48.45$, which again works out at precisely 11 to 10 in favour of the 3–3 break. In other words, there is still a 52.4% chance that the suit will break 3–3.

Familiarity with such calculations will help to keep you on the right track if you meet this sort of situation in play.

A heart is led against your contract of six no trumps. You cash the ace and king of spades (much better than ace and a low spade), but both defenders follow disappointingly with small cards.

♠ 10 9 6 2
♡ 9 7 6
◇ A Q
♣ 10 5 4 3

Still, there is a 52.4% chance that the remaining spades will be split, which gives the play of a third spade a slight edge over the club finesse.

In the first example of this chapter we saw that the probability of a 3–3 break increased less dramatically when the defenders held no significant cards in the suit. However, the position is not always clear-cut.

♠ A K 5
♡ A K Q
◇ K J 10 9 3
♣ A Q

In this case the defenders' cards are all   A K 5 4 2
equals and therefore not truly significant.   6 3
Assuming expert defence with random false-
carding, the only distributions that can be
deleted when the opponents follow to two rounds are 6–0 and
5–1. As we have seen, this gives us *a posteriori* probabilities of
57.7% for the 4–2 breaks and 42.3% for 3–3.

However, in practical play the probability of the 3–3 break is
rather higher than that. The reason is that it is often hard for a
defender to appreciate that his cards are insignificant. Suppose,
for example, that this is the position.

       A K 5 4 2

J 10 8   Q 9 7

         6 3

East, no matter how expert, is unlikely to realise that his queen and his seven are equals. It is highly improbable that he will play his queen on the first round, or even on the second. And if the queen does not appear, the probability of the 3–3 break edges up towards 50%.

The operation of the deletion principle, and the effect when a significant card is missing, is further illustrated in the two examples below.

    (a)   A K 8 7 4   (b)   A K J 7 4

         6 5 3 2   6 5 3 2

For a change, the defenders have only four cards in the suit. In
example (a), when both opponents have followed to one round
the only distribution that can be deleted is 4–0, leaving a
comparison between 3–1 and 2–2, with probabilities in the ratio
of 49.74 to 40.70, or 11 to 9. That means that at this point in time,
after both have followed to one round, there is a 45% chance that
the suit will break 2–2.

In example (b), when both defenders follow with small cards

on the first round, we can delete not only the 4–0 distributions but also the 3–1 divisions where the singleton is the queen (2 out of 8 cases). This gives us odds of 40.70 to 37.305, or precisely 12 to 11, in favour of the 2–2 break. In percentage terms this is again over 52%.

LENGTH AND SHORTAGE

What else may happen in the course of the play to modify the probabilities of distribution? Well, if it causes us to revise our calculations when the defenders follow suit with low cards, it must surely have an even more stimulating effect when a defender shows out.

This is indeed the case. When a suit is known to be divided unevenly between the defenders, the probabilities relating to the other suits undergo dramatic changes. This follows inevitably from the finite limitations of the game. Each player is restricted to thirteen cards, and a player with length in one suit has less room in his hand for cards of the other suits.

This may strike you as a self-evident truth, but don't dismiss it on that account. The concept of the amount of space available in the defenders' hands is vital to a genuine understanding of the odds in play. In their exhaustive treatise on probabilities, "The Mathematical Theory of Bridge", Emile Borel and André Cheron named this proposition the "law of attraction". Taking an analogy from the field of electro-magnetism, where like poles repel and unlike poles attract, the authors point out that length and shortage at bridge correspond to the unlike poles. Length in one suit tends to attract shortage in another. In like manner, shortage in one suit tends to attract length in another. Length repels length, and shortage repels shortage.

The experienced player, familiar with the elementary logic of distribution, is able to make good use of his knowledge in cases like this.

With no adverse bidding, South eventually becomes declarer

♠ K 10 6 5
♡ K 3
◇ A 7 3
♣ A 7 6 4

♠ A Q 8 4 3
♡ A 6
◇ K 8
♣ K Q 10 2

in six spades. West leads the jack of diamonds, and when dummy goes down South sees that there is a good chance of seven. Being a careful player, however, he resolves to make sure of the small slam. How should he proceed after winning the first trick with the king of diamonds?

The contract will be defeated only if a trick is lost in both black suits. Although there is no indication of length or shortage in the defenders' hands, South can arrive at the correct line of play by a process of hypothetical reasoning.

The spade position is such that South can pick up four trumps in either enemy hand, but he has to take a view as to where the void is more likely to lie. In clubs there is no view to take, just a one-way finessing position. A club trick will be lost only when East has a singleton or void in the suit. But if East is short in clubs it is highly unlikely that he will be void in spades as well. This is obvious to an experienced player even if he has never heard of the law of attraction. Accordingly, South leads a low spade from hand at trick two, catering for the possibility that *West* is void.

The full hand shows the distribution that South is guarding against.

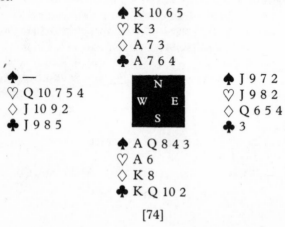

♠ K 10 6 5
♡ K 3
◇ A 7 3
♣ A 7 6 4

♠ —
♡ Q 10 7 5 4
◇ J 10 9 2
♣ J 9 8 5

♠ J 9 7 2
♡ J 9 8 2
◇ Q 6 5 4
♣ 3

♠ A Q 8 4 3
♡ A 6
◇ K 8
♣ K Q 10 2

[74]

The king of spades wins the second trick and the trumps are picked up by means of two finesses against East. The only loser is a club. If East had shown out on the first trump lead, South could have been virtually certain of losing no club trick.

Information about a defender's length in a suit may come from the bidding.

You play in four hearts after East has opened with a pre-emptive bid of three diamonds. West leads the queen of diamonds, East overtakes with the king and you win with the ace.

♠ Q 7 5
♡ A 10 7 6 3
♢ 8 2
♣ 10 9 5

Having a loser in each of the side suits, you need to bring in the trumps without loss. When you lead the queen of hearts West plays the five. What should you do?

♠ K 9
♡ Q J 9 8 4 2
♢ A 6 5
♣ A 3

The *a priori* probability of a 1–1 split is 52%, against 48% for the 2–0 divisions. Nothing has happened in the heart suit to alter these odds. We can delete the cases where West is void and where he has the singleton king, but we are left with the possibilities of 5 opposite K (26%) and K 5 opposite void (24%). So is it still a 52% shot to play for the drop? No, of course not. The fact that East is marked with long diamonds makes a big difference. As we shall see shortly, on the assumption that East has seven diamonds the probability of dropping the king is no better than 35%. The odds are nearly two to one in favour of the finesse.

Alternatively, the indications of length and shortage may emerge in the course of the play.

♠ J 9 4
♡ A K Q 7 4
◇ 7 6 5 3
♣ 5

♠ A 10 8
♡ 8 3
◇ A K 8 2
♣ A K 6 3

West leads the seven of clubs against your contract of three no trumps. East plays the jack and you win with the king. Since there will be no problem if the diamonds behave reasonably, you start with the ace and king of that suit. Unlucky! East follows once with the jack but throws a spade on the second round.

Now you have a choice between two good lines of play. You could duck a heart at once. This would ensure success whenever the hearts break no worse than 4–2, giving you an 84% chance. Alternatively, you could cross to dummy in hearts and run the jack of spades. On regaining the lead you could test for 3–3 hearts and then, if necessary, repeat the spade finesse. The probability of success for this line of play is calculated in the usual way.

Hearts 3–3	36%
At least one spade honour with East (64% × 76%)	48%
Total	84%

It looks as though there is nothing to choose between the two lines of play—until you take into consideration what is known about the distribution so far. West can be placed with length in both minor suits (his clubs are likely to be longer than his diamonds), marking East with most of the cards in the major suits. The probability of a bad heart break is therefore enhanced, and so is the likelihood that the double spade finesse will produce two tricks. These factors combine to tilt the balance in favour of playing on spades.

The next hand turned up in the international match between Scotland and England in 1978.

♠ K 10 7
♡ 10 4
◇ K 7 6 2
♣ A Q J 5

♠ 2
♡ 8 3 2
◇ J 9 4
♣ K 10 8 7 6 3

♠ A Q 9 6 4 3
♡ 9 6
◇ Q 10
♣ 9 4 2

♠ J 8 5
♡ A K Q J 7 5
◇ A 8 5 3
♣ —

E–W game
Dealer South.

England gained 11 i.m.p. by playing in a sensible contract of three no trumps while the Scots struggled in a hopeless slam.

But the main point of interest in the hand lies in what might happen if South plays in four hearts.

West leads his singleton spade, discards a club on the second round, ruffs the third spade and switches to a trump. South wins in hand and plays a second trump to dummy's ten. How should he continue?

On the face of it, a ruffing finesse in clubs gives a 50% chance of success, but declarer should realise that the 6–1 spade break has altered things. West is marked with nine cards in the minor suits and East with only five, so the ruffing finesse is well against the odds.

However, because of the known imbalance in the minors, a minor-suit squeeze against West has become a much more attractive proposition. South should therefore ruff a club and run the rest of his trumps, discarding two diamonds and a club from the table. West is unable to keep protection in both minor suits and the game is made.

[77]

One further example.

♠ Q 7 3
♡ Q 10 5
◇ A 9 6 5
♣ 10 6 2

♠ A 6 4
♡ 9 7
◇ K J 10 8 3
♣ A K 5

The contract is a cheeky three no trumps and West leads the ten of spades—a card that in his methods promises one higher honour in the suit. You play low from dummy and receive a pleasant surprise when East plays the king—an obvious singleton.

Winning the trick, you play a diamond to the ace and return a diamond. The defenders both follow with low cards on the first round, and East produces the remaining low diamond on the second round. Should you finesse or play for the drop?

Originally the probability of a 2–2 diamond split was 40.7%, but some of the diamond distributions have now been ruled out. Are you therefore entitled to apply the *a posteriori* figure of 52% for the drop—a figure arrived at by comparing the probabilities of Q x opposite x x and x opposite Q x x?

No, you know better than that, for something has happened not only in diamonds but also in spades. West's known length in spades will tend to attract a shortage in diamonds, and the finesse is now much the better chance.

How much better? That calls for a new chapter.

7

Vacant Places

It is useful to know that the odds can change substantially when there are long suits about. A basic understanding of how the law of attraction operates will save you from going wrong in many situations. But you may feel the need for a little more precision. To what extent do the odds change in such circumstances? Is there any practical way of working out the true odds when you have to make a critical decision at the table?

There is, in fact, a simple method based on normal counting technique. Consider for a moment what happens when you count out a hand. Imagine that have a two-way finessing position in spades, as shown in this diagram, with your contract depending on a correct guess.

♠ A J 5

♠ K 10 3

Naturally you delay the spade decision for as long as possible, playing on the other suits in an attempt to get a count of the hand. Suppose you eventually discover that West must have started with five spades and East with two. In the absence of any indication from the bidding, the probability of either defender holding a particular card in a suit is directly proportional to the number of cards he was dealt in the suit. The odds are therefore five to two that West holds the queen of spades, and you give yourself the best chance by taking a second-round finesse through West.

Note that the odds are not affected if both defenders play small cards under the king. Nor does it make any difference if West has discarded a couple of spades on the other suits. It is the number of cards in the suit *dealt* to each defender that matters, not the number each holds at the critical moment.

It is less generally appreciated that this counting process can be applied in reverse. Suppose the first thing you discover about a hand is that West started with five spades and East with two. Now the probability of either defender holding a particular card outside spades is directly proportional to the number of non-spades he was dealt. West, holding five spades, has eight vacant places for the cards of the other suits. East, with only two spades, has eleven vacant places. The odds are therefore eleven to eight in favour of East holding any specified card in another suit.

This proposition is of such significance in practical play that it deserves to be set out in the form of a rule.

When the distribution of one suit (or more) is completely known, the probability that an opponent holds a particular card in any other suit is proportional to the number of vacant places remaining in his hand.

Consider this hand.

Partner propels you into seven spades, and West leads the queen of diamonds to your ace. It takes three rounds to draw the trumps, East discarding three diamonds.

♠ A K 7 6 2
♡ K Q 5
♦ 7
♣ K 10 3 2

The trump distribution is known, and a count of vacant places puts West with ten and East with thirteen. The odds are therefore 13 to 10 that East has the queen of clubs.

It would be incorrect to argue that you have seen three spades and a diamond from West and four diamonds from East, giving odds of 9 to 9,

♠ Q J 9 8 3
♡ A 8
♦ A 4
♣ A J 7 4

or evens, on the location of the queen of clubs. The diamonds cannot be taken into account because the distribution of the suit is not completely known. East had to discard something on the spades, and he surely had plenty of diamonds to spare.

You will of course eliminate the red suits before committing yourself in clubs, but if both defenders follow suit it will make no appreciable difference to the odds, which will remain at 13 to 10 on East having the queen of clubs.

However, there could be a dramatic turnabout if someone were to show out. Suppose that West were to discard a diamond on the third round of hearts, giving you the complete distribution of a second suit to take into account. West would be known to have started with three spades and two hearts, leaving him with eight vacant places. East would be marked with no spades but six hearts, leaving seven vacant places. The odds would then be 8 to 7 on West having the queen of clubs.

The big advantage of this "vacant places" method is that it enables us to carry out calculations at the table without getting involved with large numbers. Is the method accurate? Yes, it is, because the whole science of probabilities at bridge revolves around the concept of the limited amount of space available in each player's hand. Can we reconcile the method with the table of *a priori* probabilities? We can do more than that. Using the "vacant places" technique we can build up the probability table from scratch.

Suppose there are a number of trumps out against you. Each opponent has an equal chance of receiving the first one that is dealt. Let us consider the 50% zone where the first trump goes to East. Now there are only twelve vacant places in the East hand against thirteen in the West hand, so East has only twelve chances in twenty-five of receiving the second trump. The probability of his receiving both trumps is 12/25 of 50% = 24%, which agrees with our figure for the 0–2 break in the probability table.

Now, if we drop a third trump into the slot, East, with only eleven vacant places in his hand, has eleven chances in twenty-four of receiving it. The probability of his receiving all three trumps is 11/24 of 24% = 11%, which again tallies with what the probability table tells us about the 0–3 break.

Similarly, East has ten chances in twenty-three of receiving the fourth trump when that is introduced. The probability that he will receive four trumps out of four is therefore 10/23 of 11% = 11/230 = 4.78%—just what the table tells us.

What about a 1–3 split? The chance that West receives the fourth trump is 13/23 of 11% = 143/2300 = 6.22%. But this is just one of the four possible 1–3 divisions of the enemy trumps. The total probability of the 1–3 split is 143/575 = 24.87%—again in precise agreement with the table.

It is not necessary to go on, for we have a sufficient indication that our calculations are valid.

THE CRITICAL SUIT

The "vacant places" method can be used not only when the distribution of a side suit is known but also when the only information comes from the critical suit itself, provided that the location of all the small cards in the suit is known.

Here is a common position.

Both defenders follow with low cards to the king and queen, and West plays the remaining low card on the third round.

♡ A K 10 4

♡ Q 7 3

In this situation it is as though the heart jack and the small hearts belonged to different suits, since neither defender would play the jack as long as he had a lower heart to play.

So, knowing the complete distribution of the small-heart suit, you are entitled to use a vacant place calculation to determine the probable location of the honour card. West, with three small hearts, has ten vacant places; East, with two small hearts, has eleven vacant places, giving odds of 11 to 10 that the jack of hearts will drop under the ace. The probability of 52.4% for the 3–3 break is arrived at more easily by this method than by going back to the *a priori* figures and comparing the frequency of J x x x opposite x x with that of x x x opposite J x x.

We can therefore qualify our "vacant places" rule as follows:

The critical suit may be included in a vacant places calculation when the location of all the small cards is known.

This gives us a simple way of solving some of the problems we considered in the last chapter. For example:

A 10 9 8 3

K 2

Both opponents follow with small cards when you cash the king and the ace. Now you have seen all the small cards and only the two honours remain. If West (say) has the queen, he will have ten vacant places to East's eleven, making the odds 11 to 10 on East having the jack. Again this gives a probability of 52.4% for the 3–3 break.

We are ready to re-examine the hand from the end of the last chapter.

♠ Q 7 3
♡ Q 10 5
◇ A 9 6 5
♣ 10 6 2

♠ A 6 4
♡ 9 7
◇ K J 10 8 3
♣ A K 5

West makes a Roman lead of the ten of spades against your contract of three no trumps. You play low in dummy and the king pops up. After winning the trick you cross to the diamond ace and return a diamond, the defenders following suit with low cards.

We concluded that, because of West's known spade length, the finesse was a better shot than the play for the drop.

Now we can work out the exact odds. Two suits can be admitted to our vacant place calculation—spades, where the distribution is completely known, and diamonds, where we have seen all the small cards. West is presumed to have six spades and has followed to one diamond, leaving six vacant places in his hand. East, who has played one spade and two diamonds, has ten vacant places. At the moment of decision, therefore, the odds are precisely ten to six, or five to three, that East has the queen of diamonds. In percentage terms, the finesse offers a $62\frac{1}{2}\%$ chance of success.

[83]

We may also take another look at the four-heart contract from page 75.

East opens pre-emptively with a bid of three diamonds and you end up as declarer in four hearts. West leads the queen of diamonds, East overtakes with the king and you win with the ace. When you continue with the queen of hearts, West plays the five.

♠ Q 7 5
♡ A 10 7 6 3
♢ 8 2
♣ 10 9 5

```
    N
 W     E
    S
```

♠ K 9
♡ Q J 9 8 4 2
♢ A 6 5
♣ A 3

Now you can work out the exact odds in the heart suit. Starting from the reasonable assumption that East has seven diamonds for his pre-emptive bid, you place West with the one diamond and the solitary small heart that you have seen. That leaves West with eleven vacant places to East's six, and the odds are therefore eleven to six in favour of taking the finesse. The probability of dropping the king of hearts under the ace has fallen from 52% to 35%—all because of East's pre-emptive bid.

Of course, in this case you cannot be absolutely certain of the diamond count. If East has pre-empted on a six-card suit, as players sometimes do, it makes a difference, but not enough to influence your line of play. The heart finesse is still a heavy favourite at ten to seven on.

♠ K 9 5 3
♡ A Q 7 6
♢ J 6 3
♣ Q 7

```
    N
 W     E
    S
```

♠ A J 8 4
♡ K 4
♢ 10 2
♣ A K J 9 3

North-South game.
Dealer South.

S	W	N	E
1 C	—	1 H	2 D
2 S	—	4 S	all pass

Vacant Places

West leads the eight of diamonds to his partner's queen. East continues with the ace, West following with the four, and then the king of diamonds. You ruff with the eight of spades, but West over-ruffs with the ten and returns the ten of hearts. East follows with the two of hearts and you win with the king.

On the ace of spades West plays the two and East the six, and when you continue with the four of spades West produces the seven. What should you do?

It is easy to do the wrong thing here. Many players would go up with the king, reasoning that the *a priori* probability of Q 6 with East (3.39%) is greater than that of singleton 6 (2.83%). But this argument ignores the evidence of diamond length with East. In such situations the only reliable guide is the comparison of vacant places—the method that takes account of the law of attraction as well as the *a priori* probabilities.

West has shown up with two diamonds and three spades. His hand contains eight vacant places where the queen of spades may be lurking. East, who has admitted to six diamonds and a spade, has six vacant places in his hand. The odds are therefore exactly eight to six, or four to three, that West has the queen of spades. By finessing the nine of spades, in other words, you will succeed 57% of the time.

A further source of possible error on this hand is the fact that we have seen a heart from each of the defenders. There is a temptation to include these cards in the vacant place calculation, which would give us odds of seven to five in favour of the finesse. But this would be incorrect because the complete distribution of the heart suit is not known. West's heart lead gave us no significant information apart from the fact that neither opponent is void in hearts. The effect of this is so small as to be negligible, and the odds remain four to three in favour of the finesse.

Sometimes a hypothetical count of vacant places will tell you what to do.

♠ J 10 4 3
♡ Q 8 2
◇ 10 9 7 4
♣ J 8

Game all.
Dealer North.

	W	*N*	*E*	*S*
		—	1 S	3 H
	all pass			

♠ K 9 5
♡ A J 10 9 6 5
◇ 6
♣ A K 3

West leads the six of spades to his partner's ace and East continues with the eight of spades. You put in the nine, but West ruffs with the three of hearts, puts his partner back on lead with the ace of diamonds, and ruffs a third spade with the four of hearts. He then exits with the king of diamonds which you ruff.

Having lost four tricks, you are faced with the problem of avoiding a trump loser. East does not need to have the king of hearts for his opening bid, but if he does have the guarded king the only way to pick it up would be to enter dummy with a club ruff in order to take the finesse. The danger is that you might suffer an over-ruff on the third round of clubs.

Before committing yourself, try projecting the play forward in your mind. Suppose that East follows to three rounds of clubs and plays the last of the small hearts when you lead a trump from dummy. West will be marked with one spade and two hearts, leaving him with ten vacant places (again you must avoid the mistake of including the incompletely-known minor suits). East will have shown five spades and one heart, leaving him with seven vacant places. The odds will therefore be ten to seven against the trump finesse.

Since the odds will favour playing for the drop in any event, you may as well cash the ace of hearts at once, thereby avoiding all risk of an over-ruff in clubs.

The full hand may be as follows:

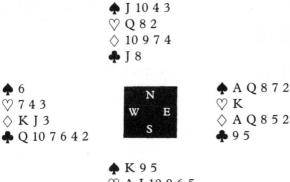

Now we are equipped to make a more accurate assessment of the odds on the hand from page 26, where we had a straight choice between two lines of play.

♠ 7 4
♡ 7
◇ A K Q 8 6 5 4
♣ A J 3

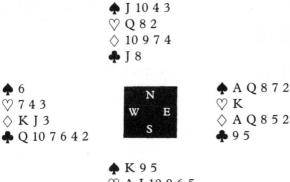

West led the five of hearts against your contract of three no trumps. East won with the ace and returned the two of hearts to the queen and king. You discarded a spade from dummy, and then a diamond as West continued with the three of hearts to the nine and jack.

The hearts appeared to be 5–4, and you had to choose between running the queen of clubs or going up with the ace and relying on the diamonds for your tricks. Using the *a priori* figures, you decided that the latter play at about 39% (35½% for

♠ A K 9 5 2
♡ Q J 6
◇ —
♣ Q 10 7 4 2

the diamond break plus $3\frac{1}{2}\%$ for the chance of finding a singleton king of clubs) was distinctly inferior to the 50% club finesse.

We mentioned at the time that the true difference between the two lines of play was quite a bit less than 11%. Two factors combine to narrow the gap. In the first place if you assume, as you are entitled to do from the play, that the hearts are 5–4, the probability of a 3–3 diamond break is immediately enhanced. Using the $_nC_r$ formula we can compare the number of hands West may have containing five hearts and three diamonds with the total number of hands he may have containing five hearts. The ratio is $_6C_3 \times {}_{11}C_5$ to $_{17}C_8$, which works out at 9240 to 24310, giving a probability of 38% for the 3–3 diamond break. Add on $3\frac{1}{2}\%$ ($62\% \times 5.66\%$) for the chance of finding a singleton king of clubs, and we have a total of $41\frac{1}{2}\%$ for the play of a club to the ace.

What is more, the assumption that West has five hearts and East four leaves West with only eight vacant places to East's nine. This means that the odds are nine to eight in favour of East holding the king of clubs. With the probability of a successful club finesse reduced to 47%, the difference between the two lines of play becomes a mere $5\frac{1}{2}\%$.

You may find it surprising that a simple assumption about a normal suit division can affect the probabilities to such an extent. It is particularly interesting to note that when one suit is known to break fairly evenly the probability of an even break in another suit is increased. This is a point worth bearing in mind for it has a general application. As the play of a hand progresses with nobody showing out, the likelihood of an even break in a critical suit increases all the time. As an extreme example, suppose that you and dummy have seven spades and that the early play shows the other suits to be breaking evenly. By trick ten, if nobody has discarded a spade, probability gives way to certainty. The spades *must* be breaking 3–3.

We can, in fact, add a rider to the law of attraction. Length attracts shortage, shortage attracts length, *and equipartition tends to attract equipartition.*

Suppose you have to play a contract of six diamonds on these cards.

♠ K Q 7 3
♡ Q
♢ K Q 6   Game all.
♣ A K J 10 2   Dealer North.

	N	
W		E
	S	

	N	*S*
	1 C	1 D
	2 S	3 H
	4 NT	5 H
	6 D	—

♠ 6
♡ A 9 8 4
♢ A J 10 9 4 3
♣ 7 5

West leads a trump, East follows and you win with the nine. When you lead the six of spades to the king, East wins with the ace and plays a second trump. The diamonds prove to be 2–2, making you wish you had drawn trumps and discarded your spade loser on the third round of clubs. Now you cash the queen of spades for a heart discard, ruff a spade, return to dummy with the king of clubs and ruff the fourth spade, both defenders following.

Both defenders play low clubs when you continue with a club to the ace, and on the jack of clubs East produces the remaining low club. What are the odds?

Everyone has followed suit so far and the distribution seems to be fairly even. West has produced four spades, two diamonds and two clubs, and has five vacant places in his hand. East has produced one extra card—the last of the low clubs—and has only four vacant places. The odds are therefore five to four in favour of ruffing the third club. The equipartition in spades and diamonds has brought the probability of the 3–3 club break up to nearly 56%.

THE EFFECT OF THE LEAD

One other occasion for using a vacant places calculation is when you can extract a valid inference from the opening lead. You are on safe ground when the lead provides an immediate indication of length and shortage.

♠ 9 4
♡ K Q 5
◇ A 7 6 3
♣ K J 10 5

You open one no trump, partner raises to three, and West leads the two of diamonds. You play low from dummy and capture East's jack with your king.

It is a fair presumption that West has led from a four-card suit, in which case he will have nine vacant places to East's twelve. The odds are therefore 4 to 3 that the queen of clubs is with East, and after a club to the king you should finesse on the way back.

♠ Q 10 5
♡ A 2
◇ K 9 5 4
♣ A 9 6 2

More difficult to assess are the inferences that arise when a defender leads an honour card. Consider this hand.

♠ 7 6 4
♡ J 7 3
◇ A J 9 4 3
♣ A Q

♠ A 10
♡ Q 10 6
◇ K 10 8 2
♣ K J 9 4

North deals and bids one diamond. Anxious to get home to bed, you jump to three no trumps, and West leads the king of spades.

On the reasonable assumption that West has the three spade honours, the odds are 13 to 10 on East holding any other card. So you win the second spade, play a diamond to the ace, both following, and unblock the clubs. If nobody shows out, and if East plays the last small diamond on the next round, you can place West with three spade honours and one diamond, East with two diamonds, and the odds are 11 to 9 in favour of finessing in diamonds.

But suppose, on the same hands, that you are the dealer and the bidding goes:

Again West leads	S	W	N	E
the king of spades,	1 C	—	1 D	—
conveying the same	1 NT	—	3 NT	all pass

message about the
spade honours.

But this time the bidding, or rather the lack of it, carries a message about the small spades. If West had held two or more of the small spades along with his K Q J (and possibly a heart honour), he would surely have made an overcall of one spade. The evidence of the bidding suggests that most of the small spades will be with East. This restores the balance of the position, and you have no special reason to do anything but play for the drop in diamonds.

The difference in the first situation is that West had no opportunity of introducing a spade suit at a reasonable level in the bidding.

The inferences are even less secure in slam contracts. Suppose that in the last hand, holding the ace of hearts instead of the queen, you find yourself playing six diamonds on the lead of the king of spades. Now you can no longer rely on West for the jack of spades. Moreover, if West does have K Q J and knows you to be inflexible of mind, he can crucify you by leading the king of spades when he has the queen of diamonds and the jack of spades when he has not.

We suggest caution, therefore, in drawing deductions from the lead of an honour card. It is hard evidence of length or shortage that is needed for vacant place calculations.

8

Freedom of Choice

In the situations that we have encountered so far we have been concerned almost exclusively with the distribution of the opponents' cards. We have not felt the need to take the human factor into account—to investigate the probability of cause or motive. Yet there are times when we need to know which of two causes (two possible defensive holdings) is more likely to have produced an observed effect (the appearance of a particular card). We need to determine, in other words, the probability that a defender will play a particular card if he has it.

Let us quickly reassure those who fear that it will make the task of calculating the odds extraordinarily difficult if the defenders' motives have to be taken into account. In the first place, it is only in certain well-defined situations that we need concern ourselves with a defender's choice of card. Secondly, the adjustment required is quite straightforward.

The odds have to be revised only when a defender, in following suit or winning a trick, has a free choice between cards which he knows to be equals—two adjacent honours such as the king and the queen, for instance. Now there is no reason to suppose that the defender will first play one card rather than the other; it is a fifty-fifty chance. The probability that he will hold the king and queen and play the queen first is therefore half of the total probability that he will hold the king and queen. The other half of the time he will play the king first. In the typical situation where free choice operates, the opponents will usually have a good idea of what is going on, and will endeavour to make their carding as uninformative as possible, whatever their normal conventions.

Let us consider a practical example.

♠ 6 4
♡ A Q 7 4
◇ A K Q J
♣ A J 10

♠ A K 5
♡ 8 6 3
◇ 10 8 7 4
♣ 7 5 2

West leads the ten of spades against your contract of three no trumps. East plays the seven and you win the first trick with the king.

At trick two you play a club to dummy's ten. East wins with an honour and returns the two of spades to your ace. Now you have a choice of finesses for your ninth trick. You can either repeat the club finesse, or you can try a finesse in hearts instead. The heart finesse you know to be a straight 50% shot. What about the club finesse? Is that also 50%?

The problem can be solved with the help of the deletion principle. You knew from the start that there was a 52% chance of finding the club honours divided, a 24% chance of finding them both with East, and a 24% chance of finding them both with West. Has anything happened in the club suit to eliminate any of these possibilities? Of course it has. East produced an honour card, so it is no longer possible for West to have both honours. The remaining possibilities are that the honours are divided (52%) or that East has them both (24%). The odds are therefore 52 to 24, or 13 to 6, that the second club finesse will win. That's a 68% chance, and the second club finesse is clearly superior to the heart finesse.

Perhaps you are wondering why we said that East won the first club with "an honour" instead of specifying which one. The vagueness was deliberate, but we are quite prepared to stipulate that East won with (say) the queen. Now someone is sure to argue as follows:

"Ah, but if East won with the queen, half of the occasions when the honours are split are also eliminated. You are left with only the 26% zone where West has the king and East the queen, so the odds are just 26 to 24 in favour of the second club finesse."

This argument is not too hard to refute. It is true that if East wins with the queen the chance of split honours is reduced by half, but so is the chance that East has both honours. Holding the king and the queen, two cards that he knows to be equals, East has the choice of winning with either card. Following our usual rule for compounding probabilities, we have to multiply the *a priori* probability that East has both honours (24%) by the probability that he would play the queen rather than the king (50%). This gives us odds of 26 to 12 in favour of the second club finesse—68% as we calculated originally.

Thus we have two different ways of arriving at the same answer. We can either half close our eyes so that we are unable to distinguish between the king and the queen, noting merely that East plays "an honour" on the first round of clubs. This gives us a straight comparison between the *a priori* probabilities of split honours and both honours with East. Alternatively we can keep our eyes wide open and observe that East plays the queen of clubs. This halves the probability of split honours, and we have to apply our understanding of the operation of free choice to halve the probability of East having both honours.

This principle has such a wide application in the play of the cards that it may be as well to set out a definitive rule for adjusting the odds in "free choice" situations.

Freedom of Choice

When a defender follows suit or wins a trick with one of two equivalent cards, the probability of his having both cards is halved.

The subject has been examined in print by several writers—by Alan Truscott in the "Contract Bridge Journal", by Borel and Cheron in the second edition of their "Mathematical Theory of Bridge", and by Terence Reese in "The Expert Game". The underlying principle—an application of Bayes' Theorem to practical card play—has come to be known, confusingly, as "the principle of restricted choice". One can see how the name originated. In the last hand, when East has the queen of clubs but not the king his choice of play is restricted. He can either win the first trick with the queen, or play low and allow you to score your ninth trick immediately. With both club honours, however, East has a free choice of two cards with which to win the trick. In general he will pick his card at random, winning half of the time with the queen and half of the time with the king. That is why, when he produces one honour or the other, only half of the total probability of the holding can be counted.

The term "restricted choice" is an unfortunate one. Apart from associations with the straitjacket and the madhouse, the overtones of complexity are such that many players refuse to make any effort to understand what is basically a very simple idea. Besides, to talk about "restricted choice" is to put the emphasis in the wrong place. It is not the restricted choice of the player who holds one honour card but the free choice of the player who holds two that necessitates an adjustment of the odds. We shall continue to refer to "free choice", therefore, in an effort to keep things logical.

You may still be unconvinced about this random choosing of a card by East. Would you, or the stolid citizens you habitually play with, really behave in this scientific way? In the cases that matter, we believe that you would. Imagine yourself in the East seat on the hand from page 93.

♠ 6 4
♡ A Q 7 4
◇ A K Q J
♣ A J 10

North opens one heart, South responds one no trump and North raises to three no trumps. The lead of the ten of spades goes to the king, and South leads a club to dummy's ten.

♠ Q J 7 2
♡ J 9
◇ 6 5 3
♣ K Q 8 3

Now it must be clear to you that the key question is what declarer will do when in hand with his last entry, the ace of spades. Will he try a heart finesse, which you know will succeed, or will he repeat the losing club finesse? Surely you will win the first club with the honour card that strikes you as the most crafty choice. What is more, for fear of being type-cast, you will not win with the same card every time you meet this situation.

Now we return to the problems of the declarer. Here is a situation that is familiar to everyone.

You play low to dummy's jack and East wins with the king. When you regain the lead and play another card from hand, West plays low. Should you put up the queen or finesse the nine?

Q J 9

6 3 2

Most players know from experience that it is better to play the queen. Why should this be so? The short answer is that East, holding both ace and king, might equally well have won the first trick with the ace. The likelihood of his having both honours is therefore halved, and again we have a probability of about 68% for the play of the queen compared with 50% for the finesse of the nine.

Suppose you are playing a contract of three no trumps with nine top tricks to run as soon as you gain the lead. Naturally the defenders attack your weak suit, shown in the diagram.

7 6

Q 10 3

When West leads the four, East wins with the ace

and shoots back the five. Should you play the ten or the queen?

Suspecting that East is trying to pull a fast one, you may be tempted to go up with the queen. Let us examine the problem dispassionately. There is no danger if the suit is divided 4–4, and if West started with five cards headed by the king and jack there is no hope. The only cases in which your choice of card is crucial are those where West has led from three cards headed by an honour—from K x x or J x x. Initially these holdings have an equal probability, but the situation changes when we take East's actions into account. If West led from K x x, East had no choice but to win the first trick with the ace. If West led from J x x, however, East had a free choice of cards and might have won the first trick with the king rather than the ace. The probability of the latter holding is therefore halved, and the play of the ten is twice as good as the play of the queen.

Of course, familiarity with your opponents' foibles may alter your view of the position. If you know that East *always* wins with the ace when he has both top honours, and if you cannot bear the thought of being outwitted, you may decide to go up with the queen after all. But if you are wrong, partner will demand to know why you went against the odds.

In the next example you can afford to lose only one trick in the suit.

You play a low card to the ace, West following with the ten and East with the five. On the next round East plays the eight. Should you put in the nine or the queen?

A 4

Q 9 7 6 3 2

You can forget about the possibility of the ten being a singleton, for you must always lose two tricks when the suit breaks 4–1. What you have to determine is whether West's ten is more likely to have come from a holding of K 10 or J 10. *A priori* these holdings have an equal probability, but free choice comes into the picture once the ten has been played. With J 10 West would have played the jack half the time, so only half of the probability of this holding can be counted. The play of the nine is therefore twice as good as the play of the queen

FINESSE OR DROP

A knowledge of the probability of cause can give practical help in those situations where an opponent drops an honour card on the first round of the suit, leaving you to decide between taking a second-round finesse and playing for the drop.

A 10 9 7 4 3

K 8 2

The play of the king draws the five from West and the queen from East, and on the next round West plays the six. Do you finesse or not?

A simple count of vacant places indicates odds of 12 to 11 on the jack being with East. But you must also take into consideration the probability that the observed effect (the fall of the queen) was produced by each of the two possible causes—singleton queen or doubleton queen-jack with East. Now you know that if East had Q J the probability of his playing the queen was only 50%, so the proportional number of 12 given by the count of vacant places has to be reduced to 6. If East has the singleton queen, however, the probability of his playing the queen (barring a revoke) was 100%. The proportional number of 11 therefore stands, and the odds are 11 to 6 that the jack is with West. In other words, the finesse is nearly twice as good as the play for the drop.

Again you may prefer to approach the problem from another angle. Imagine that the light is dim and that you have left your glasses at home. When East follows to the first round you can see that he has played an honour card but you can't make out which one. It doesn't matter in the slightest. All you need do is compare the *a priori* probability of East holding a singleton honour with that of his holding Q J doubleton. The answer is 12.44 to 6.78, which is the equivalent of 11 to 6.

In such situations you may think you can do better if you know your opponents well.

Let us have a look at the possibilities.

East holds   Proportional number

Q J	12
Q	11
J	11

Clearly, if you always finesse when East drops an honour on the first round you will succeed 22 times out of 34.

If East is a creature of rigid habit, it is possible to do slightly better. Suppose you know that East will *always* false-card with the queen when he has doubleton Q J. You can take advantage of this by going up with the ace on the second round whenever the queen appears on the first round, suceeding in twelve cases. When East drops the jack it must be a singleton, so you take the finesse, succeeding in eleven further cases for a total of 23 out of 34. You would adopt the reverse procedure if you knew that East always played the jack from doubleton Q J.

But the advantage is slight and you would need to be very sure of your man. East has only to vary his normal style of play twice out of the twelve times when he holds Q J to put you in a losing position. In practice, few players can be relied on for absolute consistency in their false-carding. Sooner or later a defender learns that his optimum strategy is to pick a card at random from two equals. That way he can expect to come out on top twelve times out of thirty-four, which is the best he can do.

Equally, declarer cannot really expect to succeed more often than twenty-two times in thirty-four, and his optimum strategy is always to finesse on the second round.

Suppose we give the defenders an extra card in the suit.

West plays low and East drops the jack   A 10 9 7 4
when you cash the king. On the second round   K 8 2
West follows with another small card. What
are the chances for the finesse and the drop?

Since you can place all the small cards with West, a count of vacant places will serve for the first part of your calculation. This gives odds of 12 to 10, or 6 to 5, that the queen is with East. But when you make the adjustment for East's free choice of card when he has Q J, this turns into odds of 5 to 3 that West has the queen. Once again the finesse is a heavy favourite.

If you are unsure about the validity of your conclusions in these situations, it is always a good idea to go back to the *a priori* probabilities for a check. The answers must tally if your calculations are correct. When we compare the *a priori* probability of singleton queen or jack with that of doubleton Q J, we get the same ratio—5.65 to 3.39 = 5 to 3.

Here is a situation that arises quite frequently in play.

         You play low to dummy's queen and return the
K Q 9 4   four to your ace, East dropping the ten on the
         second round. On the third round West follows
A 5 3   with the remaining small card. Should you play
         the nine or the king?

The count of vacant places gives odds of 11 to 10 that East will have the jack, but again we need to make an adjustment for freedom of choice. With J 10 x East might equally well have played the jack on the second round. The odds therefore become 10 to $5\frac{1}{2}$, or 20 to 11, in favour of the finesse.

This time we leave you to check the answer for yourself by comparing the *a priori* probability of J x or 10 x with that of J 10 x.

THREE EQUALS

It sometimes happens that there are three equivalent cards out against you. When this is the case our rule of adjustment has to be extended as follows:

[100]

When a defender has followed suit or won tricks with two out of three equivalent cards, the probability of his having all three cards is reduced to one-third.*

A 10 9 7

8 3 2

Needing two tricks from this suit and having no outside entry in dummy, you duck the first round to East's queen. On regaining the lead you duck a second round to East's king. On the third round of the suit West plays the remaining low card. What are the chances?

The count of vacant places indicates odds of 11 to 10 in favour of East having the jack but, as always, you need to make an adjustment for freedom of choice. Holding K Q J, East might equally well have won the first two tricks with two other combinations of cards—Q J or K J—instead of K Q. The probability of this holding must therefore be divided by three, making the odds 10 to 11/3, or 30 to 11, in favour of the finesse.

Don't take our word for it. Check for yourself by comparing the *a priori* expectation of K Q, K J and Q J with that of K Q J.

In practice the problem of three equivalent cards arises more often in this sort of situation.

A Q 8 4

K 5 3

On the first two rounds of the suit East follows with the nine and the ten. When you continue by leading towards dummy's A 8, West plays the remaining low card. Now the position is similar to that of the previous example. Holding J 10 9, East might have played J 10 or J 9 on the first two rounds instead of 10 9. This holding therefore carries only one-third of its original weight, and the odds are 30 to 11 in favour of taking the finesse.

* More generally, when a defender has followed with r out of n equivalent cards the probability of his having all n cards is reduced by the factor $_nC_r$.

IS THE FINESSE ALWAYS RIGHT?

The success-rate of the finesse appears to be improving all the time, and it is tempting to conclude that the finesse must always be the superior play in these finesse-or-drop situations. Certainly, when a defender drops one of two touching honours on the first round of a suit there is a strong presumption that his partner is likely to have the other honour. You will not go far wrong if you always take the finesse in such circumstances.

But there are exceptions and it is useful to be able to recognise these when they come along. It has to be remembered that the odds are affected not only by the probability of cause but also by the law of attraction. On some hands we see a tug-of-war with these two forces pulling in opposite directions. The only reliable way of determining the true odds at the moment of decision is to count vacant places and then make any adjustment that is required for freedom of choice.

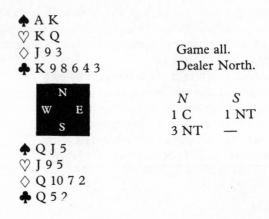

♠ A K
♡ K Q
♢ J 9 3
♣ K 9 8 6 4 3

Game all.
Dealer North.

♠ Q J 5
♡ J 9 5
♢ Q 10 7 2
♣ Q 5 2

N	S
1 C	1 NT
3 NT	—

West leads a heart against your contract of three no trumps. East wins with the ace and returns a heart to dummy's king. You play a low club to the jack, queen and ace. West perseveres with a third heart, on which dummy discards a diamond and East a spade. When you play another club West produces the seven. What should you do?

If you make the wrong decision here the defenders will have at least five tricks. Does the finesse give the better chance? This would be true if we were considering the club suit in isolation, but on this hand we also know something about the heart suit and that inevitably affects the odds in clubs.

West is known to have started with six hearts and has produced two clubs, which leaves only five vacant places in his hand. East, who has shown two hearts and one club, has ten vacant places. (The spade that East discarded on the third round of hearts is not a significant card and must not be included in our calculation. East had to part with something, and he would hardly throw the ten of clubs if he had it.) But with J 10 doubleton in clubs, of course, East might equally well have played the ten on the first round. Making the necessary adjustment, we are left with an unhelpful ratio of 5 to 5.

In this case all that science can tell you is that you must follow your nose. The finesse is just as good as, but no better than, the play for the drop.

The correct action in these situations can be reduced to a rule of thumb if we let H stand for the number of vacant places in the hand that drops an honour card in the critical suit and L for the number of vacant places in the hand that follows with low cards. Now, when the moment of decision arrives:

If $H < 2L$, take the finesse.

If $H > 2L$, play for the drop.

If $H = 2L$, spin a coin, for it is a fifty-fifty chance.

Try it out on this hand.

Match-point pairs

Game all. Dealer East.

♠ Q 7 6 4
♡ A Q 9
♢ K 6
♣ A 8 7 6

East opens with a bid of three spades, you try four diamonds and partner raises to six diamonds.

	N	
W		E
	S	

You ruff the spade lead and play a diamond to the king, West playing the queen and East the two. When you continue with the six of diamonds East plays the eight. Do you finesse the nine or play the ace?

♠ —
♡ K J 2
♢ A 10 9 7 5 4 3
♣ K Q 4

The contract is safe either way, but naturally you wish to give yourself the best chance of the overtrick. If you consider the diamond suit on its own, the odds heavily favour the finesse. However, East is likely to have a seven-card spade suit for his vulnerable three-bid, and this factor has to be taken into account.

Putting East with seven spades as well as the two diamonds we have seen leaves him with four vacant places. West, with two spades and one diamond, has ten vacant places. Since H is greater than 2L you know that it must be right to play for the drop. After the adjustment for free choice has been made, the odds are 5 to 4 that West has the jack of diamonds.

When two out of three equivalent cards have dropped, H has to be greater than 3L before it is right to play for the drop.

Freedom of Choice

♠ A K 8 7
♡ 10 9 3
◇ A J 5 2
♣ J 9

♠ Q 3 2
♡ A 7 4
◇ K Q 9 4
♣ Q 7 5

You play in three no trumps after West has bid hearts. You allow the king of hearts to hold the first trick, but take your ace when East discards a club on the second heart. West discards the ten of clubs on the second round of diamonds, and East drops the nine and the jack under the ace and queen of spades. When you play a third spade West follows with the remaining low card in the suit. What are the odds?

West is known to have started with six hearts, one diamond and three small spades. He therefore has three vacant places. East, with one heart, four diamonds and two spades, has six vacant places. Adjusting for free choice, we get odds of 3 to 2 in favour of finessing the eight of spades.

Now suppose that West follows to two rounds of diamonds before discarding. The revised count of vacant places puts West with two and East with seven. This time H is greater than 3L, and the odds are 7 to 6 in favour of playing for the drop in spades.

9

Free Choice Variations

We saw in the last chapter that when a defender plays one of two equal cards it immediately halves the probability that he has both cards. We were working mainly with honours, and it may not be clear to everyone that the principle also applies to small cards.

When a defender has a number of small equivalent cards, he has a free choice of plays. A player free from addiction to "count" signals will normally select a card at random, and the probability of his holding all the small cards is therefore reduced according to the number of choices open to him.

Here is a simple situation.

A Q J 8 5

10 9 7 6 2

Needing to avoid a loser in this suit, you lead the ten on which West plays the three. What are the chances for the finesse compared with the drop?

Everyone knows that the finesse is the better play to begin with, but many players, aware that the odds can change with every card that is played, are genuinely uncertain about the new position. Some are inclined to argue that East is just as likely to have the singleton king as the singleton four, and go up with the ace on that premise. The reasoning is incorrect, however.

Four of the eight distributions that were originally possible have now been excluded. Here are the four that are still possible.

	West	East	Proportional Number	Adjusted for Free Choice
(1)	K 3	4	13	13
(2)	4 3	K	13	$6\frac{1}{2}$
(3)	3	K 4	13	13
(4)	K 4 3	—	11	$5\frac{1}{2}$

The proportional numbers are taken directly from the *a priori* probability table.

In (1) and (4) the finesse is the winning play. The play of the ace succeeds in (2), and in (3) you must lose a trick no matter how you play.

Now compare (1) and (2). Although these holdings have the same *a priori* expectation, the position changes as soon as West plays the three. In (1) West had no choice but to play the three; he could not play the king without giving the show away. In (2) West might have played the four instead of the three, and the probability of this holding is therefore halved. The same applies in (4). Again West could have played the four rather than the three and again the probability is halved.

Thus, in the situations where our play matters, we have odds of $18\frac{1}{2}$ to $6\frac{1}{2}$, or 37 to 13, in favour of the finesse.

In the last chapter we saw that we could arrive at the answer by refusing to distinguish between honour cards. We can do the same here by paying no attention to the rank of the small cards, treating them all as x's. This "dim light" technique provides a useful alternative way of squaring up to many free choice

problems. It has the advantage of liberating you from the strain
of trying to make deductions from the defenders' actions, which
only too often will be coloured by a desire to put you off course.

Using this method, when West plays the three you register
merely that he has played an x and continue to work with the
a priori probabilities.

	West	*East*		*Probability* (%)	
(1)	K x	x	(two cases)	26	(2 × 13)
(2)	x x	K		13	
(3)	x	K x	(two cases)	26	(2 × 13)
(4)	K x x	—		11	

The figures that we extract from this comparison are exactly
the same. The finesse will succeed 37 times for every 13 times
that you find the singleton king with East.

In these situations it is not necessary for the small cards to be
adjacent in rank. Defenders tend to play insignificant cards at
random, treating them as equals even when they are not.

Test yourself in this slam contract.

♠ A K 6
♡ K 9 4
◇ A K Q
♣ Q 8 6 3

Game all.
Dealer North.

N	S
2 NT	3 C
3 NT	6 C

♠ Q 7 4
♡ A Q 5 2
◇ 6 5
♣ A J 9 4

West leads a diamond, and when dummy goes down you see that six no trumps might have been safer. At the second trick you lead the three of clubs to the two, jack and king. West puts dummy on lead with another diamond. How do you play?

There is no danger unless you run into a 4–1 trump break, and a casual player might assume that it is a blind guess whether to play the queen or the ace of clubs on the second round. Is not a singleton king with West just as likely as a singleton two with East? *A priori*, yes, but not in the light of what has happened. If West had the singleton king, East with 10 7 5 2 might equally well have played the five or the seven on the first round. The fact that he played the two reduces the probability of this holding to one-third of its original value, making the play of the ace of clubs on the second round three times as good as the play of the queen.

Again you may find it easier to regard all the small clubs as x's, and reflect that if you play the ace on the second round you will fail only when the club distribution is K opposite 10 x x x (one of the ten possible 4–1 divisions). If you play the queen of clubs on the second round, you will lose when the clubs are distributed K 10 x x opposite x (*three* of the ten possible 4–1 divisions).

Here is a similar position.

Needing three tricks from this suit, you start with a low card from hand to the six, king and ace. The argument is identical. With 10 7 6 4, West would have a free choice of three cards to play on the first round. This holding therefore carries only one-third of its original weight, and the play of the queen on the second round is three times as good as the play of the jack.

$$K\ Q\ 8\ 5$$
$$J\ 9\ 3\ 2$$

Sometimes you have to make an adjustment for freedom of choice on the part of both defenders.

Needing three tricks in the diagram overleaf, you start with a

A 9 8 3

K 10 6 2

low card to dummy's eight. This stands to gain immediately if West has both honours. But let us suppose that West plays the four and East wins the trick with the jack. Now you have to decide whether to cash the ace or the king on the next round. The ace will gain if West started with a singleton four, the king if East started with a singleton jack.

Well, if West had a singleton four he had no choice on the first round, but East might have won with the queen instead of the jack. The probability of this holding is therefore reduced to one half of its original value. If East had the singleton jack he had no choice, but West might have played either of the other two low cards on the first round. So this holding retains only one third of its original weight, and the odds are three to two in favour of playing the ace on the second round.

The answer is reached with less effort, perhaps, by reflecting that there are three outstanding low cards and two outstanding honours. The probability of a low singleton with West is therefore greater than that of a singleton honour with East in the ratio of three to two.

Familiarity with the probability of cause can help to protect you against false-carding by the defenders.

♠ J 4
♡ Q 8 7 4
◇ Q 7 2
♣ A K 8 3

♠ A K Q 3
♡ K 6
◇ A J 8 4 3
♣ 7 5

Partner is a little too enthusiastic in the bidding and you find yourself playing six diamonds on the lead of the jack of clubs. You win in dummy and lead the two of diamonds to the five, jack and nine. How should you continue?

The answer to that question depends largely on the company you are keeping. For the moment we shall assume that the defenders are competent and experienced.

There are two reasonable courses of action. You could either cash the ace of diamonds in the hope of felling the king on your right, or you could cross to dummy in order to lead the queen of diamonds, hoping to pin the ten in the West hand.

Let us set out the distributions that give you a chance.

	West	*East*
(1)	10 9 6	K 5
(2)	10 9	K 6 5

These holdings have an equal *a priori* probability, and in each case West has a choice of two equivalent cards to play on the first round. We assume in (1) that a competent West would never play the six—the card that gives you no chance to go wrong. It is one of those mandatory false-carding situations known to all players of experience. So West's choice of card cannot affect the relative probability of the two holdings.

What about East? In (1) East has no option but to play the five on the first round, whereas in (2) he has a free choice between the five and the six. The appearance of the five on the first round, therefore, is twice as likely to have been caused by a holding of K 5 than by a holding of K 6 5, and the correct play is to continue with the ace of diamonds at trick three.

However, the answer is different if a player of limited experience occupies the West seat. If West is not up to playing high from 10 9 6, your only chance is to cross to dummy and lead the queen of diamonds.

With certain combinations, each defender may have a free choice of equals to play at the same trick.

Suppose this is the trump suit, in which you can afford to lose no more than two tricks. When you lead the six from dummy, East plays the nine and West captures your queen with the ace. After regaining the lead, should you continue with the jack or a low card?

6

Q J 8 7 4 3 2

[111]

There is no way of holding the losers to two tricks if the suit is breaking 4–1, so we need consider only those 3–2 divisions that give you a chance.

	West	East
(1)	A K	10 9 5
(2)	A K 5	10 9
(3)	A 10 5	K 9

All three cases have the same *a priori* expectation. In (1) we can again assume that an experienced player in the East seat would always play the nine or the ten, never the five. Thus East had a choice of two equals to play, and so had West, who might have won the first trick with the king rather than the ace. In all, the defenders had four ways in which to play their cards, and this combination therefore retains only a quarter of its original weight.

The same applies in (2). Again the defenders had four ways of playing their cards, and the probability of the holding is reduced to a quarter.

In (3), however, the defenders had no option but to play their cards as they did. This combination therefore retains its full weight, and the odds are $1\frac{1}{4}$ to $\frac{1}{4}$, or 5 to 1, in favour of playing a low card on the second round of the suit.

This time it makes only a slight difference if you judge East to be incapable of playing high from 10 9 5. Even when (1) is ruled out as a possible holding, the odds are 4 to 1 on the play of a small card on the second round.

Considerations of free choice will not always tell you what to do in these "obligatory false card" situations.

K J 3

A 9 5 2

You finesse the jack successfully and continue with the king, West playing the four and then the queen. What now?

If West is a beginner it will be safe to finesse the

nine on the third round. But a player of any experience in the West seat, holding Q 10 4, would drop the queen—the card he is known to hold—on the second round, since that is the only way of offering you a losing option.

It is no good looking to East for help. He has the same choice of three equivalent cards to play whether he holds 8 7 6 or 10 8 7 6. Unless he is a dedicated signaller of distribution, you can read nothing into his choice of cards.

In the absence of any other indication, all you can do is fall back on the *a priori* figures (or a vacant place argument), which tell you that Q 10 4 is more probable than Q 4 in the ratio of 1.78 to 1.61, or 11 to 10.

Your respect for a defender's capability may be severely tested in the next example.

Needing to avoid a loser in this suit, you start with the ace on which East drops the queen. How do you continue?

J 8 4

If the queen is a true card, you must finesse dummy's eight on the next round, but a good

A K 9 6 3

defender might have dropped the queen from Q 10 doubleton, realising that this was the only way to give you a chance to go wrong.

Again nothing can be gleaned from West's choice of card. No matter what his holding, West had three small cards to choose from. Looking at the *a priori* position, you see that the odds are 6 to 5 in favour of East having the ten. However, from the defender's point of view, the advantages of the false card are not so obvious as in the previous example.

Unless East is an expert and the bidding has made it clear that you have the king as well as the ace, you would be well advised to take a second-round finesse after all. And even an expert should not be accorded too much respect.

FREE CHOICE ON LEAD

The odds can be affected not only by a defender's choice of card but also by his choice of suit. This hand comes from a women's knockout team event in the U.S.A.

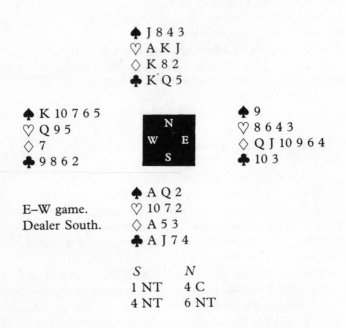

```
                    ♠ J 8 4 3
                    ♡ A K J
                    ◇ K 8 2
                    ♣ K Q 5

♠ K 10 7 6 5                        ♠ 9
♡ Q 9 5              N              ♡ 8 6 4 3
◇ 7             W         E         ◇ Q J 10 9 6 4
♣ 9 8 6 2            S              ♣ 10 3

                    ♠ A Q 2
E–W game.           ♡ 10 7 2
Dealer South.       ◇ A 5 3
                    ♣ A J 7 4

                    S       N
                    1 NT    4 C
                    4 NT    6 NT
```

West led the nine of clubs to dummy's queen. Declarer took a losing spade finesse, and West continued with a club to the king. South played a spade to the ace, finessed the eight of spades and cashed the jack, West discarding three diamonds while South threw a heart. Two rounds of clubs followed, dummy discarding a diamond and East two hearts. After a heart to the ace, declarer played off the king and ace of diamonds, forcing a discard of the last spade from West and leaving this two-card ending:

[114]

With a complete count of the hand, declarer knew East to have the master diamond and one heart left. She also knew that West started with three hearts and East with four.

When West followed with the nine of hearts at trick twelve, declarer had to decide whether the finesse would work or whether East had, in fact, been squeezed in the red suits. According to the report, she "went with the percentages" by playing the king.

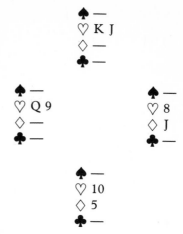

Did declarer go with the percentages? At first glance the odds appear to be 4 to 3 on East having the queen of hearts (since she was dealt four hearts to West's three), but that is before the opening lead is taken into account. Presumably West would never lead away from the king of spades and would see no attraction in the lead of the singleton diamond. Her choice of lead therefore lay between hearts and clubs. If she had held nothing but small cards in both suits, she might equally well have led a heart initially. The probability that West began with three small hearts is therefore halved.

If West had the queen of hearts, however, a club would be her only passive lead. This holding therefore retains its full weight, and the true odds are 3 to 2 on West having the queen of hearts.

10

Surveying the Scene

In this final chapter it seems fitting to review the principles that have been established and the techniques that have been learned, putting our subject in perspective against the larger canvas of the game. There is a need to warn against the danger of trying to extend any principle beyond its range of validity.

We have covered a lot of ground since we first set foot on the icy slopes of Mount Probability. Now the summit is in sight, though still far above us and wreathed in mist. Looking back, we have a clear view of the route we have climbed to reach this sunlit ridge, and from our vantage point we can identify some of the hidden crevasses that may ensnare those who follow behind us.

Far off in the distance lies our base camp, where we prepared for the journey by examining the number of ways in which a pack of fifty-two cards can be distributed between four players. The most important point to emerge from Chapter 1 is that, assuming a random deal, all specific distributions are equally likely *a priori*. The qualifying clause perhaps needs some elaboration.

RANDOM DEALING

A random deal is possible only after an efficient shuffle. At the bridge table the shuffle is often perfunctory, with the result that the cyclic pattern formed by the cards in the previous deal is not completely broken up. Then, in the deal that follows, all specific distributions will *not* be equally likely. The odds will slightly be loaded against the unbalanced distributions and in favour of the flatter hand patterns. This is one of the reasons why even breaks seem to occur rather more frequently than the table of probabilities predicts. The other reason is that when the opponents fail to contest the auction, or subside at a low level, their hands are unlikely to be wildly unbalanced.

Players taking part for the first time in a tournament where the hands are computer-dealt are sometimes surprised by the apparent skittishness of the hands, and come away grumbling about singleton honours, voids, and seven-card suits. They tend to blame the computer for their disasters, which is about as sensible as blaming bad weather on the government. A computer properly programmed for random dealing will produce hands that conform closely to the table of hand-pattern expectancy shown on page 17. It is not the computer-dealt hands but the familiar table-dealt hands that are slightly abnormal. Some experts make allowance for this factor by bidding with more aggression when the hands have been dealt at the table than when they are faced with computer-dealt hands.

THE PROBABILITY TABLE

In Chapter 2 we made a detailed study of the probable division of the opponents' cards *a priori*. In spite of our reservations about random dealing, the table on page 20 is our only secure guide, and it is quite accurate enough for normal purposes. On many hands a knowledge of the *a priori* probabilities will be all you need to make an informed choice between two plausible lines of play.

Try to memorise only the main features of the table. You will find the full table invaluable for constant reference, not only in *a priori* situations but also for certain *a posteriori* calculations where it is used in conjunction with the deletion principle, free choice, and the "dim light" technique.

The general finessing rule on page 23 gives useful guidance in those *a priori* situations where you have to choose between taking a first-round finesse and trying to drop an honour card.

PERCENTAGE PLAY

Safety and percentage play within a single suit were the subjects traversed in Chapter 3. Although space was somewhat limited, enough examples were given to show how probabilities are calculated in a wide variety of card combinations. One point not brought out in this chapter is that there is nothing absolute about the percentage play for a given combination of cards. Outside factors may exert an influence on the situation.

Suppose that you need three tricks from this suit. In the absence of any indications, the correct percentage play is to start with a low card from dummy to your queen. Whether the
K 10 4 3

Q 6 5 2

queen wins the trick or loses to the ace, you should finesse the ten on the next round.

But suppose you can be certain from the bidding that the ace lies with West. Now we have an entirely new situation. The best play is to lead low from hand to dummy's king and, if the jack does not appear, duck on the way back. This method gains over the normal percentage play when West has A x x or A x (six of the twenty 3–2 combinations) and loses to it only when West has A J x (three cases out of twenty).

By all means learn the percentage play for each combination of cards in isolation, but remember that such learning must not be applied rigidly. When you meet a combination within the context of a complete hand you have to make use of all the inferences that are available. What the opponents do, or fail to do, will often provide a clue to the correct play.

COMBINING CHANCES

Still working from *a priori* figures, we went on in Chapter 4 to examine ways of combining chances in more than one suit. Our guides over this terrain were the two laws governing the compounding of probabilities, and we had to choose the appropriate one according to whether the contract depended on the union or the intersection of two chances. This is all fairly basic and straightforward, but essential reading for anyone who hopes to make such calculations for himself.

There is a question here about how much we should attempt to work out at the table. In comparing the chances of two lines of play, how far should we go in trying to snatch a little extra percentage in our favour? Are small differences worth bothering about?

Well, there are really two different situations to consider. If there seems little to choose between two independent lines of play, the general uncertainties of bridge are such as to make it a waste of time and effort trying to determine which one is marginally the better. So pick a route quickly and hope for the best. On the other hand, there is no excuse for neglecting some precaution that provides an additional chance of safety, no matter how small. Hammer in an extra piton whenever you can.

In Chapter 5 we took note of the evasive action required to avoid damage from enemy action. There is little point in adopting a line of play that has a theoretically high probability of success if a defender can lop some 20% off your chances by attacking an option when he gains the lead. As far as possible the play should be planned so as to preserve all your chances.

CHANGING ODDS

For many readers the most interesting and rewarding section of the journey will be from Chapter 6 onwards, where we dealt with *a posteriori* calculations. As the gradient increased, the first climbing aid to be brought into use was the deletion principle. When a trick or two has been played in a suit and nobody has shown out, we can delete the unbalanced distributions which are no longer possible and recalculate the odds by comparing the *a priori* probabilities of those distributions that are still possible. This may bring about a dramatic change in the probability of an even break.

We also studied the effects of the law of attraction—the way in which length in one suit tends to attract shortage in another. This is something that a player who has any appreciation of the structure of cards must feel in his bones. It is the key to the right play in many situations where you cannot get a complete count but have reason to suspect length in a particular defender's hand.

VACANT PLACES

In the next stage of our ascent we came upon a new and direct way of calculating the odds—the count of vacant places, which quantifies the law of attraction and links it automatically with the *a priori* probabilities. For practical players this will undoubtedly prove to be the most useful tool of all. The arithmetic is simple enough for the calculations to be performed at the table, and the method is foolproof as long as the rules are followed.

Disaster can ensue if you attempt to include in your calculation any cards of a suit in which you do not have a complete count. That is the equivalent of unhitching your rope on a glassy slope leading to the edge of a precipice. A suit may be included when its distribution is fully known, and the critical suit may be included if the location of all the small cards is known.

FREE CHOICE

The final obstacle we had to overcome was the probability of cause. We saw that when a defender followed suit or won a trick with one or two equivalent cards, the probability of his having both cards was halved. This provides the vital clue to the correct play in a number of situations, particularly when an opponent drops an honour card on the first round of a suit and you have to decide between finesse and drop.

Those who find it confusing to probe enemy motives can arrive at the correct answer by using the "dim light" technique, refusing to distinguish between the enemy honours (or small cards) and simply comparing the *a priori* probabilities of the distributions in question.

A potential hazard not adequately noted in Chapters 8 and 9 is the temptation to introduce free choice arguments without taking all possible causes into account.

Suppose that this is your trump suit and that you cannot afford to lose a trick. When you play the queen, East follows with a low card and West with the ten. On the next round East plays another low card. What should you do?

Q 5

A K 9 8 4 3

A finesse is needed if the ten is a singleton. That's one out of ten 4–1 distributions with an *a priori* probability of 2.83%. The holding of J 10 doubleton with West (one out of twenty 3–2 distributions) has a higher probability of 3.39%, but this has to be halved since West might have played the jack rather than the ten. At a cursory glance the odds appear to be 5 to 3 in favour of East having the jack. So should you take the finesse?

Not on your life, for there is another possible explanation for the appearance of the ten. If West started with J 10 x it would cost him nothing to drop the ten on the first round of the suit. The effect of this is to reverse the whole position. If we assume that West would *always* drop an honour from J 10 x, the odds are 12 to 5 in favour of playing for the drop (since J 10 x opposite x x is three times as likely as J 10 opposite x x x). Even if you estimate that West will drop an honour from J 10 x only a third of the time, the odds will still be 6 to 5 in favour of playing for the drop.

Another danger, which looms not only in free choice situations but in all probabilistic calculations, is illustrated in the following hand.

♠ Q 5
♡ 8 6 5 2
◇ K 9 6
♣ A K 4 3

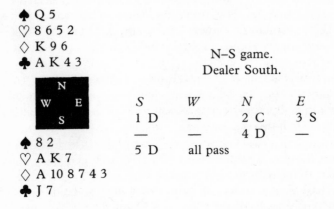

N–S game.
Dealer South.

♠ 8 2
♡ A K 7
◇ A 10 8 7 4 3
♣ J 7

S	W	N	E
1 D	—	2 C	3 S
—	—	4 D	—
5 D	all pass		

The nine of spades is led and East takes two tricks in the suit, West following with the three on the second round. East switches to the ten of clubs, covered by the jack and queen and won by dummy's king. When you play the six of diamonds from the table East puts in the queen. You win with the ace and continue the suit, West playing the remaining small diamond.

Now, on the reasonable assumption that East began with seven spades, a simple count puts West with nine vacant places to East's five. Allowance must be made for East's freedom of choice when he has both diamond honours, and the odds become 18 to 5 that the jack of diamonds is with West.

By far the best chance of avoiding a diamond loser, therefore, is to finesse the nine of diamonds. In percentage terms it is a 78% chance, but it will do you no good to avoid a diamond loser if you cannot then fulfil your contract. 78% of zero is still zero.

On this hand, after avoiding a trump loser, you still need a squeeze against West in hearts and clubs for the eleventh trick. If East has a singleton diamond, he must have at least three cards in one of these suits and the squeeze will not work.

This is therefore an occasion where you must accept the short end of the odds in diamonds, going up with the king and hoping that East's distribution is 7–2–2–2.

The lesson that has to be learned is that the best chance in a key suit does not always coincide with the best chance of making the contract. In the pairs game this process extends a stage further, for the best chance of making the contract does not necessarily represent the best chance of a good match-point score (see over).

♠ J 5
♡ K 9 5
◇ Q 8 6 2
♣ J 6 5 2

Match-point pairs

Game all.
Dealer South.

	N	
W		E
	S	

S	W	N	E
1 C	Dbl	2 C	—
—	Dbl	—	2 S
3 C	all pass		

♠ 9 2
♡ Q 8 2
◇ A K 5
♣ K Q 10 8 3

West cashes the ace and king of spades and then switches to the ace and another trump, East following. You win in hand and play the ace and king of diamonds, to which East follows with the ten and the nine. When you continue with a third round, West plays the remaining small diamond. Do you finesse or play for the drop?

On the bidding it seems reasonable to place West with four spades and East with five. You have seen two clubs and three diamonds from West, and two cards in each minor from East. That leaves four vacant places in each hand, and when we have made the adjustment for East's freedom of choice with J 10 9 of diamonds we see that the odds are 3 to 1 on West having the jack of diamonds.

The finesse therefore represents by far the best chance of making four diamond tricks and your contract. But at this stage you must ask yourself if it is necessary to make the contract when East has a doubleton diamond. Not everyone will bid up to three clubs with your cards; it is likely that most of the North-South pairs will be defending against two spades. In defence against that contract you have one club trick and possibly two hearts. If you can make no more than two diamond tricks, the contract of two spades will roll home for a score of 110. It will certainly be no tragedy if you lose 100 by going one down in three clubs when other pairs are conceding 110.

It is when the diamonds are 3–3 that you must at all costs make your contract. Two spades may then go down, and you cannot afford to give away 100 when other pairs are chalking up plus scores your way. You must therefore play for the drop in diamonds, accepting a reduced chance of making your contract in order to give yourself the best chance of a good match-point score.

. . . .

Now we leave you, relaxing in the sunshine, well trained and equipped to surmount further problems of probability as you encounter them. The principles developed in this book can be relied upon. Each has its proper place in the scheme of things and its own range of validity. But no principle can be used as a substitute for judgment. Remember always that bridge, not mathematics, is the name of the game.